11 Plus Vocabulary from Classical Roots with Prefixes/Suffixes

By

Paul Smith

Table of Contents

Section A: Introduction .... - 4 -
   (i) Plan of the book .... - 4 -
   (ii) How to use this book .... - 7 -
   (iv) Glossary .... - 10 -
Section B: Unit 1, Lesson A - Numbers 1 11
Section B: Unit 1, Lesson B - Numbers 2 21
Section B: Unit 1, Exercises 28
Section B: Unit 2, Lesson A – Shape and Size 31
Section B: Unit 2, Lesson B - Numbers 3 38
Section B: Unit 2, Exercises 45
Section B: Unit 3, Lesson A – Space and time 48
Section B: Unit 3, Lesson B – Location and Rank 56
Section B: Unit 3, Exercises 63
Section B: Unit 4, Lesson A – Body Parts 66
Section B: Unit 4, Lesson B – Age and Gender 73
Section B: Unit 4, Exercises 80
Section B: Unit 5, Lesson A – Opinions 83
Section B: Unit 5, Lesson B – Positive and Negative 90
Section B: Unit 5, Exercises 97
Consolidation 1 – Units 1-5 100
Section B: Unit 6, Lesson A – The Five Senses 103
Section B: Unit 6, Lesson B – Feelings 110
Section B: Unit 6, Exercises 117
Section B: Unit 7, Lesson A – Colours 120
Section B: Unit 7, Exercises 134
Section B: Unit 8, Lesson A – Common Verbs 1 137
Section B: Unit 8, Lesson B – Common Verbs 2 144

Section B: Unit 8, Exercises 151

Section B: Unit 9, Lesson A – Common Verbs 3 154

Section B: Unit 9, Lesson B – Common Verbs 4 161

Section B: Unit 9, Exercises 168

Section B: Unit 10, Lesson A – Adjectives, Qualities 171

Section B: Unit 10, Lesson B – Similarities and Differences 178

Section B: Unit 10, Exercises 185

Consolidation 2 – Units 1-10 188

Section C – (i)   Answers to Exercises 191

   Unit 1 191

   Unit 2 192

   Unit 3 193

   Unit 4 194

   Unit 5 195

   Consolidation 1 – Units 1-5 197

   Unit 6 198

   Unit 7 199

   Unit 8 200

   Unit 9 201

   Unit 10 202

   Consolidation 2 – Units 1-10 203

Section C (ii) – Wordlist 204

Section A: Introduction

(i) Plan of the book

Unit	Topic/skill	Roots	Exercises
(i)	How to use this book	Overview of skills covered	
(ii)		Glossary of terms List of abbreviations	
Section B: General concepts			
1. Lesson A	Numbers Introduction to roots	Numbers 1: mono, uni, bi, tri, quad, dec,	
Lesson B		Numbers 2 Penta, quin, hex, sext, numer, centum, milli, multi, null/nulla, omni	1. Sentence completion 2. Crossword 3. Multiple choice (identifying correct and Incorrect)
2. Lesson A	Shape and Size Word families, multiple roots, compounds	Shape circ, flex, glob, gon, linea, ov,	
Lesson B		Size hyper, micro, macro, mega, mid/medi, min, ultra	1. Words used correctly and incorrectly 2. Scales 3. Fill in the Blanks
3. Lesson A	Time and Space Study skills, antonyms, collocations, words often confused	Time ante, chrono, pre, post, retro, temp/per	
Lesson B		Location ad, inter, infra, intra, sub, tele, trans	1. Antonyms and collocations 2. Jumbled letters 3. Multiple choice, odd one out

Unit	Topic/skill	Roots	Exercises
4. Lesson A	The Person Study skills, roots and suffixes	Body Parts cardio, derma, manu, neur, op/t, or/oralis, ortho, osteo, ped, phys, psych	
Lesson B		Gender and Age andr, frater, ger, heter, homo, juven, mater, mort, nat, pater, soror	1. Matching roots and suffixes 2. Fill in the Blanks 3. Spidergrams
5. Lesson A	Expressing yourself Study skills, roots as prefixes	Opinions ab, anti, con, contra, pro, ora	
Lesson B	Register	Positive and Negative bene, dis/dys, il/im/in/ir, neg, prob	1. Matching prefixes 2. Collocations and register 3. Crossword
Consolidation 1 Units 1-5			Building Word-bank Writing
6. Lesson A	Senses and Feelings Study skills: write your own examples	The 5 senses aud, phon, tact, vid, vis, voc	
Lesson B	Adverbs and suffixes	Feelings ami, ego, path, phil, phobia, sens/senti	1. Synonyms and antonyms 2. Crossword 3. Sentence completion (collocations)
7. Lesson A	Everyday life More about collocations	Colours Colour/chrom, alb/aspr/leuk, melan/nigr, cirr/pyrrh/rhod, rub, aur/argent/chrys, cyan/chlor/sapphire	
Lesson B	More than one root	Transport and Travel aero, circ/cylind/helic, mob, mot, naut/nav, port	1. Labelling diagrams 2. Multiple choice 3. Fill in the Blanks

Unit	Topic/skill	Roots	Exercises
8. Lesson A	Actions Study skills: root trees	Common Verbs 1 form, migr, ati/pass, spect, tract, volv	
Lesson B		Common Verbs 2 capt/cept/ceive, miss, quer/quir, serv, struct, tort	1. Completing context tables 2. Matching definitions 3. Collocation triangles
9. Lesson A	More Actions Alternative spellings	Common Verbs 3 auto, cad/cid/cas, duc, hab, lev, mis	
Lesson B		Common Verbs 4 here/hes, jac/ject, rot, sili, syn, vers/vert,	1. Jumbled letters
10. Lesson A	Descriptive Words Study skills: visual decoding skills	Adjectives 1: properties acer, hed, dyn, fort, grav, pugn, soph, vac	
Lesson B		Similarities and Differences ambi, equi, idi, iso, sym, vari	1. Word formation 2. Context and collocations 3. Definitions and examples
Consolidation **2 Units 1-10**			Vocabulary alphabet Countable and uncountable Writing (critical thinking)
Section C: Supporting Materials			
i)	Answers to exercises		
ii)	Word list		

(ii) How to use this book

Aims

- To improve the vocabulary of students preparing for the 11 plus.
- To teach Greek and Latin roots as a tool to expand academic vocabulary.
- To encourage students to really get to know words, acquire and internalise vocabulary for use and not to simply memorise a word list.
- To teach vocabulary skills to enable students to go on to further self-study.
- Provide necessary exercises to test and consolidate learning whilst making them as varied and interesting as possible.

What does it mean to know an English word?

1. Identify the root or roots.
2. Know the meaning. This may involve both the dictionary definition (denotation) and associations of the word (connotation).
3. Understand the chain of reasoning between the classical root(s) and modern English usage.
4. Know how to spell and pronounce it.
5. Know the part of speech, e.g. noun, verb or adjective.
6. Know how to use the word grammatically correct in a sentence.
7. Know which words it does, or does not collocate with.

This book aims to teach all of these aspects of acquiring vocabulary.

Organisation of the Book

- There are 3 sections:
    Section A is the introduction and contains tips on how to use the book, a glossary and a list of abbreviations.
    Section B contains ten units each comprising two lessons, A and B. These focus on roots used in the expression of core concepts and general functions in English.
    Section C contains answers to exercises and a word list.
- Unlike many other vocabulary books, roots and derived words are not chosen at random. Each unit, and each lesson has a topic. These should help you remember the new words and use them in context.
- Each root or group of related roots has a separate page.
- There are 5 target words per page for each root or group of related roots.

> *Target words are divided into **Core words** and **Progression words.***
> *Core words are more commonly used and should be learned first. The less common, more academic progression words should then be added. Both groups are required to complete the exercises successfully.*

- Each lesson ends with points to note about the usage of roots.
- Each unit concludes with 3 exercises designed to practise the vocabulary from both lessons and the points noted.
- There are consolidation activities after every 5 units.
- Where possible target words have been recycled in definitions and examples in subsequent units. Words so recycled are shown in **bold**. Use the word list in Section C to find the original reference.

<u>Study Tips</u>

- Short periods of regular study are more effective than long irregular sessions.
- Try to set aside a period of 30-60 minutes each day and do one lesson per day.
- To learn new roots and new words:
    Study the definition, part of speech and example given.
    Try to understand the logical connection between the root and the modern usage of the word.
    Practice saying the word aloud. Phonic spelling has been included to help you with pronunciation.
    If you have a study partner try to explain to him/her what the word means.
    Try to write your own example sentence using the new word.
    Tips on additional study skills will be provided at the end of the lessons.

- Many of the words in this lesson had disputed meanings when they were first formed. Many of them still do. Some concepts, e.g. in law are understood differently in different cultures. If you do not agree with the example sentence in the book, try to make your own using the target word. If possible, ask a teacher to check it for grammar and spelling.
- When you think you know the new words, try the exercises. Do them from memory. Do not look back at the text and copy.
- Check your answers in the key in Section C. If the vast majority of your answers are correct, move on to the next unit. If not, review before moving on.
- Review what you have learned regularly. There is a consolidation after every 5 units to help you.

(iii) **Abbreviations**

Many abbreviations used in academic English are of the same Greek and Latin origin as the roots studied in this book. These abbreviations will, therefore, be used throughout the book along with standard dictionary abbreviations for English grammar and parts of speech.

(adj.)	adjective
(adv.)	adverb
c	circa (about, approximately)
cf.	confer (compared with)
e.g.	exempli gratia (for example)
G	Greek
i.e.	id est (that is)
L	Latin
(n)	noun
n (c)	noun countable
n (u)	noun uncountable
(n) (plural)	noun normally used in the plural form
N.B.	nota bene (note well)
prep	preposition
(v)	verb
v (I)	intransitive verb (can stand alone)
v (T)	transitive verb (requires an object)

(iv) Glossary

Antonyms	Words with opposite meanings, e.g. large/small.
Collocations	Words which are often used together, e.g. verb + noun, e.g. drive a car, Adjective + noun, e.g. delicious food
Context	The topic being discussed.
Core words	Words commonly used in everyday English which should be learned first.
Diphthong	Two consecutive vowels pronounced as one.
Partitive	A word which denotes quantity used to make an uncountable noun countable, e.g. a pair of binoculars, a jar of jam.
Parts of speech	Types of words with different functions in a sentence, e.g. verb, noun, adjective, adverb.
Prefix	The beginning of a word which tells you part of the meaning, e.g. **un**happy
Progression words	More challenging words. These are academic and topic specific words some of which consist of more than one root. They should be learned after the core words in this book.
Root	The source of a word carrying the main meaning, e.g. **astro**naut (astro is Latin. It means space.)
Suffix	The ending of a word which tells you part of the meaning, e.g. Japan**ese**. ...ese = denotes nationality
Synonyms	Words with the same or similar meaning, e.g. large/big.
Visual decoding skills	The ability to work out the meaning of a word from its root, prefix and/or suffix as well as the context in which it is used.

Section B: Unit 1, Lesson A - Numbers 1

Study Skills: Introduction to Roots

English was borrowed extensively from other languages, especially during the Renaissance c1450-1650 as scholars needed more words to describe new ideas and phenomena. Most of the words they borrowed were base words. That means words which convey meaning. Today they are called **roots.**

Roots were often combined with beginnings and endings of words, known as **prefixes** and **suffixes** respectively, to make new English words.

These prefixes and suffixes often give you more important information such as the part of speech (verb, noun, adjective, etc.), or whether a word is positive or negative. In this book you will learn how to use both roots and prefixes and suffixes to work out the meaning of new words, especially in reading. Teachers call the process of deducing meaning in this way, **visual decoding skills**.

You will also learn to how to recognise roots. But be careful. Not all similar spellings are roots. For example, in this unit you will learn the Latin root "tri" meaning "three" but not all words containing the letters "tri" come from this root. For example, "trial" has no connection with the root "tri".

Recognising roots, therefore, means understanding the connection between the classical root and modern English usage. This is not always obvious but these chains of reasoning can be fascinating and can shed much light on all sorts of subjects from history to science.

*The symbol * next to a word means that there is an explanation of the chain of reasoning in the Study skills section of that unit.*

Many books and websites imply that all roots in English come directly from either Latin or Greek. This is only partially true. Many roots entered the English language via other Roman languages, particularly Norman French. It is important to understand this at the outset of the course because it helps to explain the variety of spellings and pronunciations of the same root which occur in modern English. We will meet examples like "quad", "quadr" and "quadri" in Unit 1 which all mean "four".

In this book Latin roots will be marked as "Bi" **(L)** and Greek roots as "Mono" **(G)** for example. But, frankly, knowing whether a root is Latin or Greek does not help you use it correctly in modern academic English. It is more important to realise that English often borrowed roots with the same, or similar, meanings from both Latin and Greek. You will see an example in Unit 1. "Mono" is Greek, "Uni" is Latin but both mean "one" in English. <u>Understanding this can improve your range of **synonyms.**</u>

Roots were not the only academic tools borrowed from the ancient Greeks and Romans. Roman numbers are still used in some academic texts and will be used in this book to encourage familiarity. Similarly, many Latin abbreviations are used in modern academic texts, especially in references. Therefore, standard Latin abbreviations will be introduced throughout this book and explained when first used. There is also a table of them in the introduction.

Latin numbers and abbreviations introduced in this unit

i	one		ii	two
iii	three		iv	four
v	five		vi	six
vii	seven		viii	eight
ix	nine		x	ten
xi	eleven		xii	twelve
xiii	thirteen		xiv	fourteen
xv	fifteen		xvi	sixteen
xvii	seventeen		xviii	eighteen
xix	nineteen		xx	twenty
xxi	twenty one		xxii	twenty two
xxiii	twenty three		xxiv	twenty four
xxv	twenty five		xxvi	twenty six
xxvii	twenty seven		xxviii	twenty eight
xxix	twenty nine		xxx	thirty

cf.	*confer*	compared with
e.g.	*exempli gratia*	for example
N.B.	*nota bene*	note well

Vocabulary from Classical Roots

1. mono (G)   "one", "single", "alone"

Core words
monarch
monogamy
monoplane

i) **monarch** (n) (c)   **mon**-ahrk

A person who rules alone as a king or queen.

Queen Elizabeth II of Great Britain is the longest reigning <u>monarch</u> in the world.

ii) **monogamy** (n) (u)   m*uh*-**nog**-*uh*-mee

The state of being married to one person at a time.

In most Western countries, <u>monogamy</u> is required by law.

iii) **monoplane** (n) (c)   **mon**-*uh*-pleyn

An aircraft with one wing on each side of the fuselage cf. biplane and triplane.

Louis Bleriot crossed the English Channel in 1909 in one of the first <u>monoplanes</u>.

iv) **monocycle** (n) (c)   **mono**-*sai*-kl

A vehicle like a bicycle but with only one wheel.

Nowadays monocycles are used mainly for fun and entertainment but in the past, they used to be a means for serious transportation.

v) **monotheist** (adj.)   **mon**-*uh*-thee-st

Describing belief in the existence of only one God.

Christianity is a <u>monotheist</u> religion.

Progression words
monocycle
monotheist

Vocabulary from Classical Roots

2. uni (L)   "one", "single", "the whole"

Core words
- uniform
- unify
- unique

vi) **uniform** (n) (c), (adj.)   **yoo**-n*uh*-fawrm

A single style of dress worn by many people, e.g. soldiers. / Describing a body of things which are all similar in fashion.

German soldiers in World War II wore field grey <u>uniforms</u>. / Many streets in British cities have a <u>uniform</u> style of houses.

vii) **unify** (v) (T)   **yoo**-n*uh*-fahy

The action of drawing people or things together.

Garibaldi <u>unified</u> many states and cities to form the modern nation of Italy in 1870.

viii) **unique** (adj.)   yoo-**neek**

Describing something which is the only one of its kind.

Elephants are <u>unique</u> animals because they drink through a long trunk.

ix) **unilateral** (adj.)   yoo-n*uh*-**lat**-er-*uh*l

An action taken by one party to an agreement or contract without the knowledge or consent of the other(s).

Rhodesia made a <u>unilateral</u> declaration of independence from the UK in 1965.

x) **university** (n) (c)   yoo-n*uh*-**vur**-si-tee   *

An institution of higher education which has the power to confer degrees.

Harvard is considered by some to be the most prestigious <u>university</u> in the world.

Progression words
- unilateral
- university

3. bi (L) "two", "twice", "once in every two"

Core words
- bicycle
- bimonthly
- binoculars

xi) **bicycle** (n) (c)   **bahy**-si-k*uh*l

A vehicle with two wheels which requires balance by the rider.

The bicycle was invented in the early 19th century but nobody agrees who the inventor was.

xii) **bimonthly** (adj.)   bahy-**muhnth**-lee

Something which occurs once every two months.

In some companies the strategic management team meets bimonthly to decide on future policy.

xiii) **binoculars** (n) (plural)   bahy-**nok**-y*uh*-ler

An optical device with two small telescopes, held with one in front of each eye.

Birdwatchers often use a pair of binoculars to get a closer look at the birds.

xiv) **binary** (adj.)   **bahy**-ner-ee

Describing something using a number scale consisting only of the numbers 0 and 1.

Computers store information in the form of binary numbers.

xv) **binomial** (adj.)   bahy-**noh**-mee-*uh*l

A term in math to describe the probability distribution in an experiment with two possible outcomes.

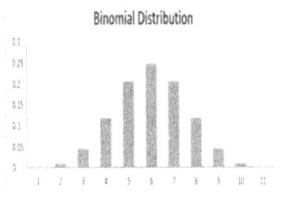

A binomial distribution is used in quality control to monitor the percentage of satisfactory products.

Progression words
- binary
- binomial

4. tri (L)   "three", "third", "three times"

Core words
- triangle
- triplicate
- tripod

xvi) **triangle** (n) (c)   **trahy**-ang-g*uh*l

A flat shape with three straight sides.

An equilateral triangle has three equal sides.

xvii) **triplicate** (n) (c), (v) (T)   **trip**-li-kit / **trip**-li-keyt

Something copied twice so there are a total of three examples. / The action of making two copies of something, cf. duplicate.

Governments often used to require official forms to be completed in triplicate.

xviii) **tripod** (n) (c)   **trahy**-pod

A stand with three legs.

Photographers often use a tripod to keep their camera steady when taking pictures.

xix) **triumvirate** (n) (c)   trahy-**uhm**-ver-it

Rule by a team of three people.

Julius Caesar, Crassus and Pompey formed a triumvirate to rule Rome from 60BCE to 53BCE.

xx) **Trinity** (n) (u)   **tri**-ni-ti

In Christianity the union between Father, Son and Holy Ghost as one God.

Medieval Christian paintings often portrayed the Holy Trinity.

Progression words
- triumvirate
- Trinity

5. quad/quart (L)   "four", "four times"

Core words
- quadrangle
- quadrilateral
- quadruple

xxi) **quadrangle** (n) (c)   **kwod**-rang-g*uh*l

A square shaped space surrounded by buildings on four sides.

Traditional Oxford and Cambridge colleges were designed as a series of quadrangles.

xxii) **quadrilateral** (n) (c)   kwod-r*uh*-**lat**-er-*uh*l

A geometrical shape having four sides and four angles.

A square is a quadrilateral in which all four sides are of an equal length and all the angles are 90°.

xxiii) **quadruple** (v), (adj.)   kwo-**druph**-p*uh*l

To multiply something by four or increase it by 400%. / Describing something which is four times the norm.

China's GDP quadrupled between 1980 and 2008.

xxiv) **quadruped** (n) (c)   **kwod**-r*oo*-ped

An animal with four feet.

Cows, horses and sheep are all common quadrupeds.

xxv) **quartet** (n) (c)   kwawr-**tet**

A group of four persons or things.

In classical music, Mozart wrote several pieces for quartets of stringed instruments.

Progression words
- quadruped
- quartet

18

6. dec (G)   "ten"

Core words
- decade
- December
- decibel

xxvi) **decade** (n) (c)   **dek**-eyd

A period of ten years.

The Beatles are often associated with the <u>decade</u> 1960 – 1969.

xxvii) **December** (n) (u)   dih-**sem**-ber   *

The last month of the year in the western, solar calendar.

The winter solstice (the shortest day) is on 21 <u>December</u> in the northern hemisphere.

xxviii) **decibel** (n) (c)   **des**-*uh*-bel

A measure of the intensity of sound using a logarithmic scale derived from base 10.

Prolonged exposure to sound at more than 85 <u>decibels</u> can lead to hearing loss.

xxix) **decimate** (v) (T)   **des**-*uh*-meyt

To kill or severely damage something in large numbers, to reduce by ten.

The Russians <u>decimated</u> the German army at Stalingrad in the winter of 1942-43.

xxx) **The Decameron** (n) (u)   De-**kam**-er-*uh* n

A work of fiction by Giovanni Boccaccio.

In <u>The Decameron</u>, written in 1353, ten survivors of the Black Death tell each other 100 stories over 10 days.

Progression words
- decimate
- The Decameron

Vocabulary from Classical Roots

N.B.

Pronunciation

The pronunciation of the same root can vary when it is used in English words, e.g. **monarch** and **monogamy**. Some books and websites claim to give you the original Latin or Greek pronunciation but this is impossible. Nobody knows how ancient Latin or Greek words were pronounced because there are no audio recordings and there were probably many local dialects. Always use modern English phonics to help you pronounce new words.

Collocations

To use root words fluently it is important to learn their **collocations**. Collocations are sets of words often used together, e.g. a noun and a verb, an adjective and a noun or a partitive and an uncountable noun. Make notes of collocations as you find them. In this lesson note:

xiii)   a pair of binoculars (**partitive** + noun)

xxvi)   decimal point, e.g. 0.25

Chains of Reasoning

x)   University: In the Middle Ages, all knowledge was believed to be part a single whole which came from God. A university was a place where students could go to study all the branches of the single whole that was knowledge and understand how they linked together in the Kingdom of God.

xxvii)   December: The Roman year began in March not January as modern years do. Consequently, December was the tenth month in the Roman calendar.

Section B: Unit 1, Lesson B - Numbers 2

1. numera (L) "number"

Core words

numerate

numerator

numerous

i) **numerate** (adj.) **noo**-mer-it

Describing somebody who is good with numbers and math.

<u>Numerate</u> people generally find it easier to get a good job.

ii) **numerator** (n) (c) **noo**-m*uh*-rey-ter

In math, the number on the top of a fraction.

In the fraction ⅔ two is the <u>numerator</u>, cf. denominator.

iii) **numerous** (adj.) **noo**-mer-*uh* s

Describing something which exists in large numbers.

Insects are the most <u>numerous</u> forms of life, accounting for about 40% of all species in the eco system.

iv) **enumerate** (v) ih-**noo**-m*uh*-reyt

To count. / To identify by name individuals or ideas when counting them.

The professor <u>enumerated</u> six reasons to support his thesis.

v) **numerology** (n) (u) noo-m*uh*-**rol**-*uh*-jee

The study of numbers with a view to determining one's future.

The ancient Greeks believed in <u>numerology</u> because they thought that numbers, such as your date of birth, influenced your destiny.

Progression words

enumerate

numerology

Vocabulary from Classical Roots

2. penta (G) / quin (L) / hex (G) / sex (L)   "five"/ "five" / "six" / "six"

<u>Core words</u>
pentathlon
quintile
hexagonal

vi) **pentathlon** (n) (c)   pen-**tath**-lon

An athletic event including five disciplines.

The <u>pentathlon</u> was the climax of the Olympic Games in ancient Greece.

vii) **quintile** (n) (c)   **kwin**-til, -tahyl

One fifth *of a population ranked by some kind of test score.*

To get into a good university in America you need to score in the top <u>quintile</u> in SAT or ACT tests.

viii) **hexagonal** (adj.)   hek-**sag**-*uh*-nl

Describing a *shape with six sides.*

Most nuts used in engineering are <u>hexagonal</u>.

ix) **quintessence** (n) (u)   kwin-**tes**-*uh* ns   *

The pure and concentrated core of a substance or idea.

Some people think that McDonalds is the <u>quintessence</u> of modern American consumer culture.

x) **sexagenarian** (n) (c)   sek-s*uh*-j*uh*-**nair**-ee-*uh* n

A person, male or female, between the ages of 60 and 69.

Most <u>sexagenarians</u> either have retired or are thinking about retirement.

<u>Progression words</u>
quintessence
sexagenarian

3. cent/centi (L) "hundred", "a hundredth"

Core words
- century
- centenary
- centimetre

xi) **century** (n) (c) **sen**-ch*uh*-ree

A period of one hundred years.

The 21st century is expected to be a time of unprecedented change.

xii) **centenary** (n) (c/u) sen-**tee**-n*uh*-ree

One hundred years after an event.

The centenary of the outbreak of World War 1, in 2014, attracted a lot of attention in the media.

xiii) **centimetre** (n) (c) **sen**-t*uh*-mee-ter

A unit of measure, one hundredth part of a meter.

I wear trousers with a waist size of 36 centimetres.

xiv) **centigrade** (n) (c) **sen**-ti-greyd

A unit of measure of temperature on a scale from 1 to 100.

All major countries except Britain and the USA use centigrade as the standard unit of temperature.

xv) **centurion** (n) (c) sen-**tyoo** r-ee-*uh* n

A Roman soldier who was a member of a unit of 100 men.

Roman centurions were the best equipped and trained soldiers in the ancient world.

Progression words
- centigrade
- centurion

Vocabulary from Classical Roots

4. milli (L) / kilo (G)   "thousand", "thousandth"

Core words
millennium
millipede
kilowatt

xvi) **millennium** (n) (c)   mi-**len**-ee-*uh* m

A period of one thousand years.

The ancient Roman Empire lasted for more than a <u>millennium</u> from around 700 BCE until the sack of Rome in 410 CE.

xvii) **millipede** (n) (c)   **mil**-*uh*-peed   *

An insect with a body made up of a large number of sections each with a pair of legs.

A lot of people think <u>millipedes</u> are scary but, in fact, most of them are harmless.

xviii) **kilowatt** (n) (c)   **kil**-*uh*-wot

A unit of measure of electrical current containing a thousand watts.

Most countries charge consumers for electricity measured in <u>kilowatts</u> used per hour.

xix) **millibar** (n) (c)   **mil**-*uh*-bahr

A unit for measuring atmospheric pressure used in weather forecasting.

Atmospheric pressure of 1000 <u>millibars</u> is normal. Lower pressures indicate bad weather.

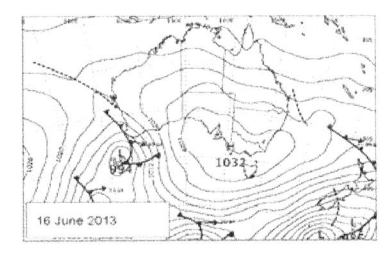

xx) **kilohertz** (n) (c)   **kil**-*uh*-hurts

A unit of measure for radio frequencies containing 1000 hertz.

Short and long wave radio bands are defined partly by the number of <u>kilohertz</u> they use.

Progression words
millibar
kilohertz

5. multi (L)   "many"

> **Core words**
> multi-storey
> multitude
> multilateral

xxi) multi-storey (adj.)   **muhl**-tee-**stawr**-ee

Describing a building having several levels.

Multi-storey car parks began to appear in British cities in the 1960s when cars first became affordable for most families.

xxii) multitude (n) (c)   **muhl**-ti-tyood

A large number of something, typically people or problems.

The Second World War created a multitude of problems for the United Nations to solve.

xxiii) multilateral (adj.)   muhl-ti-**lat**-er-*uh* l

An agreement between several parties. / Something which has several aspects.

The Paris Climate Change Accord is a multilateral treaty intended to control global warming.

xxiv) multicultural (adj.)   muhl-tee-**kuhl**-cher-*uh* l

Describing a society which aims to treat people from different cultures as equals.

London is a multicultural city but people have different opinions about it.

xxv) multifaceted (adj.)   muhl-tee-**fas**-i-tid

Describing something which can be viewed from many aspects.

Adapting to climate change is going to be a multifaceted problem.

> **Progression words**
> multicultural
> multifaceted

25

Vocabulary from Classical Roots

6. null/nulla (L), omni (L),   "zero/nothing", "all"

Core words

omnibus

annul

omnipresent

xxvi) **omnibus** (n) (c)   om-n*uh*-buhs   (Abbreviation: bus)

A vehicle used for carrying passengers. / A complete collection of the works of a writer, musician or artist.

The omnibus was invented by Georg Shillibeer in Paris in 1829. / My grandfather left me an omnibus edition of the works of Charles Dickens.

xxvii) **annul** (v) (T)   *uh*-**nuhl**

To legally declare that something never happened, or is invalid.

Henry VIII tried to annul his marriage with Catherine of Aragon on the grounds that it had been against Canon Law and was, therefore, invalid.

xxviii) **omnipresent** (adj.)   om-n*uh*-**prez**-*uh*nt

Describes something which is present everywhere.

Oxygen is omnipresent in the Earth's atmosphere.

xxix) **nullify** (v)   **nuhl**-*uh*-fahy   *

The action of giving something zero meaning or effect in law.

A contract can be nullified if one of the parties was legally unable to consent to it, e.g. because they were too young or suffering from a mental illness.

xxx) **omniscient** (adj.)   om-**nish**-*uh*nt

Having knowledge of or power over all things.

The ancient Greeks did not believe their gods to be omniscient.

Progression words

nullify

omniscient

26

N.B.

Chains of Reasoning

ix) quintessence: The ancient Greeks did not know the modern periodic table of the elements. They believed there were four known elements, earth, air, fire and water. But they did not understand gravity and so could not explain how the sun, stars, earth and moon maintained positions. To overcome this problem they conceived a mysterious fifth element, called quin, which was similar to the modern concept of energy in Astrophysics (Unit 19). The root **quin** has thus come to mean the core of something which is not immediately obvious.

xvii) millipede: The ancient Greeks and Romans did not have the same requirement for exactitude in statistics, especially large numbers, that we do today. Most large numbers, for example of casualties in battles or long distances in Greek and Roman literature, are approximations or guesses. The root **milli** is sometimes used in this sense, meaning a lot, rather than exactly 1,000. So, a millipede does not have exactly 1000 legs, just a large number.

xxix) nullify: Roman numbers were developed for trading and as you cannot buy or sell nothing, they did not have a numeral for zero. Instead they used the word **nulla** which has become the root **null** in modern English when it is usually used as a verb meaning to make something into nothing.

Vocabulary from Classical Roots

Section B: Unit 1, Exercises

Exercise 1: Sentence completion

Complete each sentence with an appropriate word from this unit. The root is given to help you and the first one has been done as an example.

1. An equilateral **triangle** (tri) is a shape with three sides each of the same length.

2. Health and safety officials monitor the number of …………….. (dec) in noisy factories.

3. Bismark ………….. (uni) a group of principalities and cities to form the nation state of Germany in the late 19th century.

4. Weather forecasts in some countries show temperature on a …………………… (centi) scale.

5. Accountants need to be highly ……………… (numer) in order to understand and communicate the meaning of the figures they work with.

6. Computer languages work by requiring the machine to make ……………. (bi) choices between zero and one representing yes and no.

7. The …………………. (quin) of a subject is defined as its essential core.

8. Christianity believes in only one God, therefore it is a ………………… (mono) religion.

9. Medieval students studied seven subjects at ………………… (uni) which were believed to comprise the whole of knowledge.

10. Most fan heaters use two or three ……………. (kilo) of electricity per hour.

Vocabulary from Classical Roots

Exercise 2: Crossword

Complete the crossword below using the clues given and words from this unit.

Across
3. A distribution of probabilities with two possible outcomes
7. A period of ten years
8. An Olympic sport with five disciplines
9. An aircraft with one wing on each side

Down
1. To multiply something by four
2. The 100th anniversary of an event
4. Describing something which exists in large quantities
5. Describing an agreement between several countries
6. To reduce by a factor of ten
9. A person who rules alone

Exercise 3: Multiple choice

Choose the best answer for each question. The first one has been done for you as an example.

1. (b) Which of the following roots means many?

    a) mono   (b) multi)   c) hex   d) milli

2. (   ) Which of the following roots can form an English word meaning a geometrical shape with six sides?

    a) sex   b) quad   c) pent   d) hex

3. (   ) Which of the following sentences is correct?

    a) To annul something means to legally state that it is invalid.
    b) To annul something means to legally approve it.
    c) To annul something means to legally declare it to be true.
    d) To annul something means to legally declare that it is valid.

4. (   ) Which of the following sentences uses the root milli <u>incorrectly</u>?

    a) A millimetre is a unit of length which represents one thousandth of a meter.
    b) A millibar is a unit of barometric pressure used in weather forecasting.
    c) Ancient Roman soldiers served in units called millenniums.
    d) A millipede is an insect with a lot of legs.

5. (   ) Which of the following words describes the condition of being married to one person?

    a) polygamy   b) bigamy   c) monogamy   d) trigonometry

6. (   ) Which of the following terms is <u>not</u> used in math?

    a) triangle   b) hexagonal   c) numerator   d) centenary

7.   ) Which one of the following roots is Greek in origin?

    a) dec   b) uni   c) numer   d) bi

8. (   ) Which of the following words describes somebody who knows everything?

    a) omnibus   b) omnipresent   c) omniscient   d) universal

Section B: Unit 2, Lesson A – Shape and Size

1. circ (L)   "round"

> **Core words**
> circulate
> circus
> encircle

i) **circulate** (v) (T)   **sur**-ky*uh*-leyt

The action of communicating something, usually a document, among a group of people. / To move something in a circular manner.

In business it is usual to circulate the agenda before a meeting. / Ventilation systems circulate fresh air around a building or a car.

ii) **circus** (n) (u)   **sur**-k*uh* s

A show involving performing animals, clowns, acrobats, etc. held in a large round tent.

A visit to the circus used to be a popular treat for children.

iii) **encircle** (v) (T)   en-**sur**-k*uh* l

The action of surrounding something or somebody.

The Chinese city of Liuzhou is almost encircled by hills which limit the available land for expansion.

iv) **circulation** (n) (c)   sur-ky*uh*-**ley**-sh*uh* n

The process of moving something around. / The readership of a newspaper or magazine.

The growing popularity of the internet means that newspaper circulations have fallen sharply since 2000.

v) **circumstances** (n) (plural)   **sur**-k*uh*m-stan-siz

The situation surrounding an event.

I think we made the best possible decision given the difficult circumstances the company finds itself in.

> **Progression words**
> circulation
> circumstances

2. linea (L)   "line"

Core words
- alignment
- delineate
- realign

vi) alignment (n) (u)   *uh*-**lahyn**-m*uh* nt

The placing of objects along a straight line. / The coordination of ideas, policies or administrative procedures.

The car was difficult to drive because the front wheels were out of alignment.

vii) delineate (v) (T)   dih-**lin**-ee-eyt

To draw, or verbally define the shape of something precisely.

Modern CFD and CAD/CAM computer programs can delineate a new product in three dimensions with great precision.

viii) realign (v) (T)   re-*uh*-**lahyn**

The action of reorganising objects or people to bring them into conformity with a standard.

The new management realigned the HR procedures in the company's many subsidiaries to bring them into conformity with international standards.

ix) curvilinear (adj.)   kur-v*uh*-**lin**-ee-er

A space bounded or defined by curved lines.

The surface area of curvilinear shapes can be challenging to calculate.

x) lineage (n) (c)   **lin**-ee-ij

The direct line of descent from a person's ancestors.

In feudal societies lineage was extremely important as it determined rights to land, titles and sometimes offices of state.

Progression words
- curvilinear
- lineage

3. glob (L) "sphere"

Core words
- global
- globalization
- global warming

xi) **global** (adj.) **gloh**-b*uh* l

Describing something which affects the entire world in some way.

Coca Cola is a global brand.

xii) **globalization** (n) (u) gloh-b*uh*-l*uh*-**zey**-sh*uh* n

The process of something, e.g. a product or a cultural practice spreading throughout the world.

In recent years the internet has increased the speed of globalization.

xiii) **global warming** (n) (u) **gloh**-b*uh* l-wawrm-ing

The process of the average temperature on Earth increasing.

Most scientists believe that global warming is the result of human activity.

xiv) **globule** (n) (c) **glob**-yool

Describing something shaped like a sphere.

Globules of fat in the blood can cause heart problems.

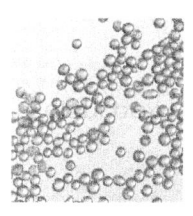

xv) **globulins** (n) (c) **glob**-y*uh*-lin

A family of proteins with globular shaped molecules occurring in plant and animal tissue.

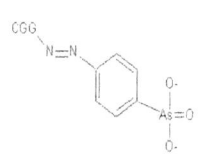

Globulins are an important part of the human immune system.

Progression words
- globular
- globulin

33

Vocabulary from Classical Roots

4. gon (G)   "corner" / "angle", "dimension"

Core words

diagonal

pentagon

octagonal

xvi) **diagonal** (n) (c), (adj.)   dahy-**ag**-*uh*-nl

A line connecting two non-adjacent angles of a shape, e.g. a square.

I like to slice my sandwich <u>diagonally</u>.

xvii) **pentagon** (n) (c)   **pen**-t*uh*-gon

A regular shape with five sides and five angles.

The headquarters of the United States Department of Defence is known as the <u>Pentagon</u> because of the shape of the building.

xviii) **octagonal** (adj.)   ok-**tag**-*uh*-nl

A regular shape with eight sides and eight angles.

MG cars always had an <u>octagonal</u> badge.

xix) **polygon** (n) (u)   **pol**-ee-gon

A shape having three or more sides and angles.

Unlike pentagons and hexagons, the sides and angles of a <u>polygon</u> do not have to be equal.

xx) **trigonometry** (n) (u)   trig-*uh*-**nom**-i-tree

A branch of math involving the study of the relationship between the the sides and angles of triangles.

<u>Trigonometry</u> was first developed by the ancient Greeks and is used nowadays for making maps.

Progression words

polygon

trigonometry

5. ov (L), rect/reg (L)   "egg", "straight"

Core words
oval
rectangular
regiment

xxi) **oval** (n) (c), (adj.)   **oh**-v*uh* l

An object with a shape similar to an egg.

The Indianapolis motor speedway is the most famous of many <u>oval</u> race tracks in the USA.

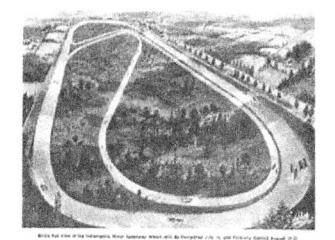

xxii) **rectangular** (adj.)   rek-**tang**-gy*uh*-ler

Describing a geometrical shape having two pairs of sides of unequal length and four right angles.

Most paintings and photographs are mounted in <u>rectangular</u> frames.

xxiii) **regiment** (n) (c)   kwo-**druph**-p*uh* l   *

A large body of soldiers.

The 51st highlanders are one of the most famous <u>regiments</u> of the British army.

xxiv) **ovulate** (v) (I)   **ov**-y*uh*-leyt

The action of producing an egg for reproductive purposes.

Pandas <u>ovulate</u> once every year.

xxv) **erect** (v) (T), (adj.)   ih-**rekt**   *

To build. / Describing something which is upright or vertical.

It takes great skill to <u>erect</u> a tall building that is perfectly vertical.

Progression words
ovulate
erect

Vocabulary from Classical Roots

6. flect (L)   "bend"

Core words
- flexible
- inflexible
- reflect

xxvi) **flexible** (adj.)   **flek**-s*uh*-b*uh*l

Describing something which can bend or adapt easily.

In modern business <u>flexible</u> working requires employees to adapt quickly and easily to different jobs.

xxvii) **inflexible** (adj.)   in-**flek**-s*uh*-b*uh*l

Something which is rigid and cannot be bent or adapted.

Steel is <u>inflexible</u> which is why it is used to build bridges and other rigid structures.

xxviii) **reflect** (v) (I) (T)   ri-**flekt**

To bend or bounce something back from a solid surface towards its source.

Radar works because radio waves are <u>reflected</u> from a solid object in their path, e.g. an aircraft.

xxix) **deflect** (v) (I) (T)   dih-**flekt**

To bend something away from its original direction of travel but not return it to its source.

Armour on a tank <u>deflects</u> incoming shells.

xxx) **inflection** (n) (c)   in-**flek**-sh*uh* n

A bend or curve in a line graph plotting change in something.

Expression of emotions causes an <u>inflection</u> in the pitch of the human voice.

Progression words
- deflect
- inflection

36

N.B.

Word Families

Many roots appear in several words from the same family, e.g. (xxx) **miniaturize**. There is also a noun, **miniature** and an adjective, **miniature**. It is very important to make notes of the part of speech of the word you are learning. You should also use a dictionary to form word family tables as you study this book.

Not all roots form words in all four main parts of speech. Do not make up words just to fill gaps.

In some cases, there may be more than one adjective, adverb or noun often using **prefixes** to indicate negative. See Unit 5 for more on this topic.

Noun	Adjective	Verb	Adverb
miniature	miniature	miniaturize	-----------
-------------	flexible	flex	flexibly
	inflexible		inflexibly

More than one root

Some **progression words** use more than one root and you need to know both to fully understand the meaning, e.g. (xx). **trigonometry**. This comprises **tri** "three" and **gon** "angle" to mean the study of the relationship between the sides and angles in a triangle.

Chains of Reasoning

xxiii)   Ancient armies nearly always fought in closely packed rectangular formations for mutual protection, hence the unit which formed such a square or rectangle became known as a regiment.

xxv)   Roman buildings were usually designed around geometric shapes, usually squares and rectangles. The Romans also built tall. Most houses in Republican Rome (1st century BCE, 2nd century AD) had five or six floors, each a rectangle built on top of the one below. This was unique in the ancient world and gave rise to a new use for the root **rect** and led to the modern English verb to **erect**.

Vocabulary from Classical Roots

Section B: Unit 2, Lesson B - Numbers 3

1. mega (G), min (L)   "great"/ "large", "less"/ "small"

Core words
- megabyte
- mini skirt
- minimum

i) **megabyte** (n) (c)   meg-*uh*-bahyt

A unit of measure for large amounts of computer memory.

The more <u>megabytes</u> of memory a digital device has, the more useful it will be.

ii) **minuscule** (adj.)   min-uh-skyool

Very small or tiny.

His salary was <u>minuscule</u> compared to his expenses and he had no savings.

iii) **minimum** (n) (c), (adj.)   min-*uh*-m*uh*m

The least possible, or least acceptable quantity of something.

Universities usually have <u>minimum</u> entrance requirements in terms of exam grades.

iv) **megalomania** (n) (u) meg-*uh*-loh-**mey**-nee-*uh*

A mental illness in which a person has a greatly exaggerated idea of their own importance and power.

Dictators such as Hitler and the ancient Roman emperor Nero are widely believed to have been suffering from <u>megalomania</u>.

v) **miniaturize** (v) (T)   min-ee-*uh*-ch*uh*-rahyz

The action of making something as small as possible.

Engineers try to <u>miniaturize</u> components in products such as mobile phones to make them as light and small as possible.

Progression words
- megalomania
- miniaturize

38

2. micro (G)   "very small"

Core words

microchip

micrometre

microscopic

vi) **microchip** (n) (c)   **mahy**-kroh-chip

A tiny piece of silicon on which are mounted millions of electronic circuits.

Moore's Law says that the power of computer <u>microchips</u> will double every two years.

vii) **micrometre** (n) (c)   mahy-**krom**-i-ter

An instrument for measuring tiny distances very accurately.

<u>Micrometres</u> are widely used in precision engineering to measure distances as small as a thousandth of an inch.

viii) **microscopic** (adj.)   mahy-kr*uh*-**skop**-ik

Describing something which is so small it cannot be seen with the naked eye but only with a microscope.

Lung diseases can be caused by breathing <u>microscopic</u> particles of pollution in the air.

ix) **microbiology** (n) (u)   mahy-kroh-bahy-**ol**-*uh*-jee

The study of microscopic forms of life.

<u>Microbiology</u> is very important for identifying new microorganisms and viruses such as HIV and Ebola.

x) **microbe** (n) (c)   **mahy**-krohb

A microorganism, usually a harmful form of bacteria.

<u>Microbes</u> cause some of the most annoying human conditions, e.g. acne.

Progression words

microbiology

microbe

3. macro / magn (L) "large", "great"

Core words
- magnify
- magnificent
- magnate

xi) **magnify** (v) mag-n*uh*-fahy

The action of making something appear bigger.

Binoculars and microscopes use lenses to magnify small objects.

xii) **magnificent** (adj.) mag-**nif**-*uh*-suhnt

Describing something which makes a great impression on the viewer by its size or quality.

The ancient Greeks and Romans carved magnificent statues to honour their heroes and Gods.

xiii) **magnate** (n) (c) **mag**-neyt

A business man or landowner with great wealth and power.

Rupert Murdoch is one of the most powerful media magnates in the world.

xiv) **macrocosm** (n) (u) **mak**-r*uh*-koz-*uh*m

The entire structure of something, e.g. the universe, cf. microcosm.

When paying attention to detail it is easy to lose sight of the macrocosm.

xv) **macroeconomics** (n) (u) mak-roh-ek-*uh*-**nom**-iks,

The study of the economy of an entire country or economic system, cf. microeconomics.

Macroeconomic policies are made by governments and deal with areas such as the money supply, interest rates, inflation and unemployment.

Progression words
- macrocosm
- macroeconomics

4. midi (L) (G) / medi (G) "middle",

Core words
- intermediate
- midway
- mediate

xvi) **intermediate** (adj.) in-ter-**mee**-dee-it

A stage between the two ends or extremes of something.

Language learners have to take <u>intermediate</u> level courses before becoming fluent.

xvii) **midway** (adj.), (adv.) **mid**-wey

The point halfway between two other places.

The Battle of <u>Midway</u> in 1942 took place on two Islands in the Pacific Ocean midway between the United States and Asia.

xviii) **mediate** (v) (T) **mee**-dee-eyt

The action of trying to resolve a conflict between two or more people often involving negotiation.

The United Nations sometimes try to <u>mediate</u> between countries in order to keep the peace.

xix) **middlebrow** (adj.) **mid**-l-brou

Describing a person with average tastes and a medium level of culture.

<u>Middlebrow</u> people are the majority in most countries; they are neither ignorant nor highly cultured.

xx) **mediocre** (adj.) mee-dee-**oh**-ker *

Describing something of average or poor quality.

Parents complained that the students test results were <u>mediocre</u> once again this year.

Progression words
- middlebrow
- mediocre

Vocabulary from Classical Roots

5. ultra (L)   "extreme", "beyond"

Core words
- ultimate
- ultimatum
- ultra-modern

xxi) **ultimate** (adj.)   **uhl**-t*uh*-mit

The highest point of a series. / The highest possible level of something.

Soldiers killed in war are said to have made the <u>ultimate</u> sacrifice for their country.

xxii) **ultimatum** (n) (c)   uhl-t*uh*-**mey**-t*uh* m

The final and most extreme of a series of demands made by one party to another during a dispute.

Britain sent an <u>ultimatum</u> to Germany to withdraw from Poland on Sept 3rd 1939. It was ignored and World War II began.

xxiii) **ultra-modern** (adj.)   uhl-tr*uh*-**mod**-ern

Describing the latest, most advanced products or ideas.

The Apple campus in Cupertino, California is an example of an <u>ultra-modern</u> office complex.

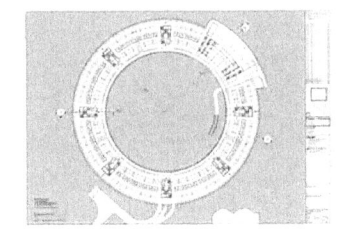

xxiv) **ultrasound scan** (n) (c)   **uhl**-tr*uh*-sound skan

A medical technique for examining the human body using sound waves at extremely high frequency.

<u>Ultrasound scans</u> have revolutionised the diagnosis of cancer and other tumours.

xxv) **ultraviolet** (adj.)   uhl-tr*uh*-**vahy**-*uh*-lit

Invisible rays having frequency higher than the violet colour.

Too much exposure to <u>ultra violet</u> radiation from the sun can cause skin cancer.

Progression words
- ultrasound
- ultraviolet

6. hyper (G) (L)   "too much", "excessive", "beyond"

<u>**Core words**</u>

hype

hyperactive

hypermarket

xxvi) **hype** (n)(u), (v)   hahyp

Excessive publicity given to something.

The fame of some pop stars is based more on <u>hype</u> than talent.

xxvii) **hyperactive** (adj.)   hahy-per-**ak**-tiv

Describing a person who is excessively active; has too much energy.

A growing number of children have Attention Deficit Hyperactive Disorder (ADHD). Nobody knows for sure why.

xxviii) **hypermarket** (n) (c)   **hahy**-per-mahr-kit

A huge retail store which sells a range of goods beyond other types of shops.

<u>Hypermarkets</u> are usually located in out of town retail parks.

xxix) **hypertension** (n) (u)   hahy-per-**ten**-sh*uh* n

A medical condition in which the patient has excessive blood pressure.

<u>Hypertension</u> is dangerous and is sometimes caused by too much stress or pressure.

xxx) **hyperventilate** (v) (T) (I)   hahy-per-**ven**-tl-eyt

A medical condition in which the patient breathes abnormally fast and deeply.

If you <u>hyperventilate</u> you will feel dizzy and may collapse. You should see a doctor immediately.

<u>**Progression words**</u>

hypertension

hyperventilate

N.B.

Compounds

Many roots are used to make new compound words, particularly in science and technology, such as:

(xv)   macroeconomics

(xxv)   ultraviolet

(xxix)   hypertension

Make lists of other examples you know using the roots we have learned so far.

Note that these compounds can be one word, hyphenated or two words. Be careful with spellings.

Where to find roots

The majority of roots come at the beginning of English words but not always. Sometimes a prefix is used and the root appears in the middle of the word, e.g. **intermediate** (xvi). See Unit 5 for more on this topic.

Chains of Reasoning

xx)   Some words in English have changed their meaning over the years but the root has not changed. One example is **mediocre**. *Med* originally meant medium or average but the word mediocre has gradually come to have a stronger, more negative meaning despite its root.

Vocabulary from Classical Roots

Section B: Unit 2, Exercises

Exercise 1: Root words used correctly and incorrectly

Are the following sentences correct or incorrect? Write (C) for correct or (I) for incorrect. Correct the wrong sentences.

1. (   ) A magnate is a businessman whose companies control a large part of an economic sector.

   ....

2. (   ) A microchip is a very large electronic circuit at the heart of a computer.

   ....

3. (   ) Steel is a very flexible material used for making car bodies.

   ....

4. (   ) A football pitch is a rectangular grass field approximately 105 metres x 75 metres in size.

   ....

5. (   ) Newspaper circumstances are dropping dramatically and some titles are now available online only.

   ....

6. (   ) The word *equivalent* is a synonym for *similar*.

   ....

7. (   ) Megalomaniacs are people who are obsessed with their own importance.

   ....

8. (   ) Children who have hypertension have too much energy and are often disruptive in school.

   ....

Vocabulary from Classical Roots

Exercise 2: Scales

1. *Complete the following scale using information from this unit.*

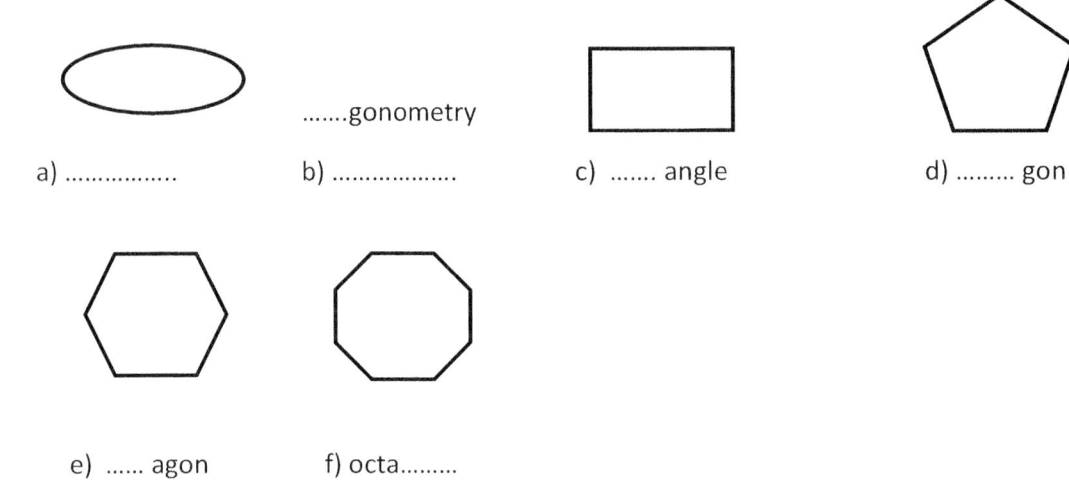

a) ....   b) ....…….gonometry   c) .... angle   d) .... gon

e) ...... agon   f) octa.........

2. *Place the words in the Word-bank in the correct order to make a scale from smallest to largest.*

a) ....   b) ....   c) ....   d) ....

e) ....   f) ....

Word-bank

ultra   mini

hyper   medi

micro   macro

Exercise 3: Fill in the Blanks

Choose the best word from the box to fill in the blanks in the following passage.

> **Word-bank**
> globulins
> circulates
> microscopic
> hypertension
> microbiology
> ultramodern
> hyperventilation
> scans

Modern medicine has largely abandoned the theories and treatments used by the ancient Greeks and Romans but still draws heavily on vocabulary formed from Greek and Latin roots. This is because many of the discoveries on which modern medicine is based occurred during the Renaissance c1500-1650 when English was borrowing heavily from Greek and Latin to form new words to describe scientific discoveries. One example is the work of William Harvey, an English scientist who discovered that blood (1) _____ around the body and is not static as the ancients believed.

But even today the names of (2) _____ treatments such as ultrasound (3) _____ are derived from Greek and Latin roots. So are the medical names for many newly discovered parts of the body such as (4) _____ which are proteins vital to the human immune system shaped like drops of water. The names of medical conditions such as high blood pressure which doctors call (5) _____ are also derived from Latin and Greek roots.

Modern science allows doctors to treat many diseases which were fatal in ancient times. For example (6) _____ allows modern doctors to identify and treat bacteria and viruses which were unknown to their ancient counterparts who believed that all illnesses were caused by imbalances between the five elements of earth, air, fire, water and **quin**. However, modern life has also given rise to a lot of new diseases. Respiratory diseases caused by breathing (7) _____ particles of pollution in the air are a particular problem. Another issue is diseases such as hypertension and (8) _____ caused by the stress of modern life.

Therefore, anyone who wants to become a doctor or nurse needs to have a good understanding of Greek and Latin roots!

Section B: Unit 3, Lesson A – Space and time

Latin abbreviations introduced in this unit

a.m.	*ante meridiem*	time before midday
i.e.	*id est*	in other words
p.m.	*post meridiem*	time after midday

1. ante (L)   "before", "in front of"

Core words
- antemeridian
- antecedent
- antediluvian

i) **antemeridian** (adj.)   an-tee-m*uh*-**rid**-ee-*uh* n   (*Abbreviation* **a.m.**)

Describing time before midday.

In some primary schools, classes start at 8 a.m.

ii) **antecedent** (n) (c)   an-t*uh*-**seed**-nt

An event or institution which took place or existed before another, usually with some relationship to the later event or institution.

The League of Nations was an antecedent to the present-day United Nations.

iii) **antediluvian** (adj.)   an-tee-di-**loo**-vee-*uh* n

Describing a person, object or behaviour which is very old and out of date.

Many young people think that their grandparents' fashion sense is antediluvian.

iv) **antenatal** (adj.)   an-tee-**neyt**-l

Describing something which occurs before the birth of a baby.

Doctors believe that regular antenatal checks during pregnancy can improve the health of mothers and babies.

v) **anteroom** (n) (c)   **an**-tee-room

A small room in front of the main rooms of a house or suite of offices.

In a traditional Chinese house visitors would wait in an anteroom before being allowed to see the master.

Progression words
- antenatal
- anteroom

Vocabulary from Classical Roots

2. pre (L)   "before", "earlier", "in front of"

Core words
previous
precedent
predict

vi) **previous** (adj.)   **pree**-vee-*uh*s

Describing something which occurred earlier than another event.

If a criminal has a previous history of similar offences, he/she will usually receive a heavier sentence.

vii) **precedent** (n) (c)   **pres**-i-d*uh*nt

A previous situation which sets a rule to be followed in the present situation.

There was no precedent for the situation in which the company found itself.

viii) **predict** (v) (T)   pri-**dikt**

The ability to foretell what will happen in the future.

The ancient Greeks believed that people called Oracles received messages from the Gods and consulting them enabled a person to predict the future. The Oracle of Apollo at Delphi was the most famous.

ix) **preface** (n) (c), (v) (T)   **pref**-is

An introduction to an academic book. / The action of introducing something.

It is quite common for a book by a new young writer to include a preface from someone more famous to explain why the book is important.

x) **pre-war** (adj.)   pre-wawr

Describing something which occurred before a war, usually in western countries before World War II.

There are a huge number of books about conditions in pre-war Germany.

Progression words
preface
pre-war

50

3. post (L)   "after", "behind"

Core words
- post-war
- postpone
- posthumous

xi) post-war (adj.)   pohst-wahr

Describing something which took place after a war, in western countries usually after World War II.

Many countries experienced a severe housing crisis in the post-war years after 1945.

xii) postpone (v) (T)   pohs-**pohn**

The action of changing the date of something to a later time.

The match has been postponed due to bad weather and will now be played next Saturday.

xiii) posthumous (adj.)   pos-ch*uh*-m*uh*s

Describing something which occurs after the death of the subject.

Jochen Rindt is the only driver to have won a posthumous Formula 1 world championship.

xiv) postgraduate (n) (c), (adj.)   pohst-**graj**-oo-eyt

A student who is studying for a further qualification after obtaining a bachelor's degree.

Nowadays more and more students think that a bachelor degree is not enough to get a good job and go on to do postgraduate study.

xv) postscript (n) (c)   **pohst**-skript

Additional material added to a book after the original version has been finished.

Writers sometimes add a postscript to the 2nd edition of a book to bring the contents up to date.

Progression words
- postgraduate
- postscript

Vocabulary from Classical Roots

4. retro (L)   "back", "backward"

Core words

retrograde

retro style

retrospectively

xvi) **retrograde** (adj.)   **re**-tr*uh*-greyd

Describing something which is believed to be a step backwards.

Some customers complain that the latest model of smartphone is a <u>retrograde</u> step in terms of size.

xvii) **retro style** (n) (c)   **re**-tr*uh*-stahyl

*A product which is deliberately made to look like something from a **previous** era.*

Some designers use <u>retro styles</u> to appeal to customers' sense of nostalgia.

xviii) **retrospective** (adj.), (n) (c)   re-tr*uh*-**spek**-tiv

Describing the action of looking back on something. / An exhibition of the work of an artist.

The <u>retrospective</u> exhibition of Picasso's drawings at the Tate Modern gallery was fascinating.

xix) **retrofit** (v) (T)   **re**-troh-fit

The action of fitting an upgraded part to a machine after it has been manufactured.

Some countries now require that power stations are <u>retrofitted</u> with devices to reduce dangerous emissions of pollution.

xx) **(anti)retroviral** (n) (c), (adj.)   **an**-tee **re**-troh **vahy**-r*uh* l

A class of medicines used to treat viral infections.

The availability of <u>antiretroviral</u> drugs has dramatically increased the life expectancy of some patients.

Progression words

retrofit

(anti)retroviral

5. chrono (G)   "time"

Core words
- chronic
- synchronize
- anachronism

xxi) **chronic** (adj.)   **kron**-ik

Describing something, usually unpleasant, which occurs continuously over a period of time.

Many former coal miners suffer from <u>chronic</u> lung diseases such as pneumoconiosis caused by breathing coal dust at work.

xxii) **synchronize** (v) (T)   **sing**-kr*uh*-nahyz

The action of arranging for two or more things to happen at the same time.

It is common for companies to <u>synchronize</u> the release of important financial information in all media e.g. newspapers, TV and social media.

xxiii) **anachronism** (n) (c)   *uh*-**nak**-r*uh*-niz-*uh*m

Something used in an inappropriate time period.

If a tank appeared in a movie about the American Civil War that would be an <u>anachronism</u>.

xxiv) **chronological** (adj.)   kron-l-**oj**-i-k*uh*l

Describing a series of events organised by order of time with the oldest first.

Many classic novels, e.g. Jane Eyre use a <u>chronological</u> narrative to hold the story together.

xxv) **asynchronous** (adj.)   ey-**sing**-kr*uh*-n*uh*s

Describing operations which take place without the use of fixed time intervals.

E-mail communication is <u>asynchronous</u> because it does not have to be read at the same time as it is sent, unlike phone calls where two people have to communicate at the same time.

Progression words
- chronological
- asynchronous

6. temp (L), per (L)   "time", "through", "throughout"

> **Core words**
> temporary
> permanent
> contemporary

xxvi) **temporary** (adj.)   **tem**-p*uh*-rer-ee

Describing something which exists for only a short period of time.

Nowadays a lot of businesses employ <u>temporary</u> workers during busy seasons of the year like Christmas.

xxvii) **permanent** (adj.)   **pur**-m*uh*-n*uh*nt

Describing something which exists throughout time; for ever.

The right to <u>permanent</u> residence means that a person can live in a country throughout their lifetime.

xxviii) **contemporary** (adj.), (n) (c)   k*uh*n-**tem**-p*uh*-rer-ee

Describing something which happens in the present period of time. / A person who lives at the same time as another.

<u>Contemporary</u> music is closely connected with fashion and lifestyle. / Winston Churchill was respected by his <u>contemporaries.</u>

xxix) **temporal** (adj.)   **tem**-per-*uh*l

Describing time.

In the social sciences, the <u>temporal</u> boundaries of a study are the time period which the research covers.

xxx) **perennial** (adj.)   p*uh*-**ren**-ee-*uh*l

Describing something which occurs regularly or permanently.

In botany, <u>perennial</u> plants are species which flower every year, e.g. daffodils.

> **Progression words**
> temporal
> perennial

N.B.

Antonyms

Many roots have been used to make pairs of English words with opposite meanings, known as antonyms. Learning these words in pairs will help you remember and use them. One useful technique is little diagrams:

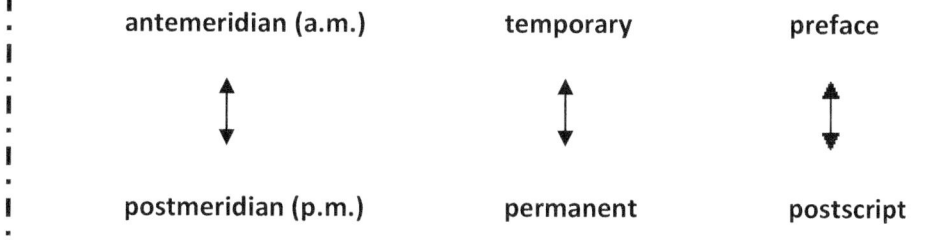

antemeridian (a.m.)	temporary	preface
↕	↕	↕
postmeridian (p.m.)	permanent	postscript

Collocations

We have mentioned collocations (words often used together) **previously.** In this unit pay attention to collocations of adjectives and nouns. When you are learning new words make notes of them with their collocations, e.g.

adj. + noun   adj. + noun

temporary worker   chronic disease

Review this lesson. How many more adjective + noun collocations can you find? Make notes.

Words often confused

If you are not familiar with Greek and Latin, it is easy to confuse some roots which have similar spelling and pronunciation. In this unit do not confuse **ante** "before" with **anti** "against" (see Unit 5).

Vocabulary from Classical Roots

Section B: Unit 3, Lesson B – Location and Rank

1. inter (L)   "among", "between"

Core words

international

interval

intersection

---

i) **international** (adj.)   in-ter-**nash**-*uh*-nl

Describing something taking place between two or more nations.

International trade increased massively following the signing of the General Agreement on Tariffs and Trade in 1948.

ii) **interval** (n) (c)   **in**-ter-v*uh*l

A space between two objects. / A period of time between two events.

In school examination rooms there is usually an interval between desks to prevent students from copying.

iii) **intersection** (n) (c)   in-ter-**sek**-sh*uh*n

Where two roads meet. / A point where two lines on a graph meet.

In economics, the intersection of supply and demand is called the **equilibrium** point.

iv) **intermission** (n) (c)   in-ter-**mish**-*uh*n

An interval between two parts of a public performance.

For many years cinemas and theatres had to have an intermission in each performance which was used to sell ice creams and drinks.

v) **interpersonal** (adj.)   in-ter-**pur**-s*uh*-nl

Describing something occurring between persons.

Good interpersonal skills are vital for communication and team working in modern business.

Progression words

intermission

interpersonal

2. intra/intro (G)   "within", "inside"

<u>Core words</u>
- introvert
- intranet
- intransitive

vi) **introvert** (n) (c), (adj.)   **in**-tr*uh*-vurt

A person who keeps their feelings within themselves.

Albert Einstein was one of the most successful <u>introverts</u> of all time.

vii) **intranet** (n) (c)   **in**-tr*uh*-net

*A network of computers connected within one institution, **i.e.** not connected to the wider internet.*

Most universities have <u>intranets</u> for staff to communicate privately with each other and with students.

viii) **intransitive** (adj.)   in-**tran**-si-tiv

A grammar term describing a verb which can be used within a sentence without an object.

Some human actions such as *smile* and *laugh* are <u>intransitive</u> verbs.

ix) **intravenous** (adj.)   in-tr*uh*-**vee**-n*uh* s

Describing something that is given inside a vein.

In medicine, an <u>intravenous</u> drip is a device for giving a patient a drug by inserting a needle into a vein for the blood to carry the medicine around the body.

x) **intrapersonal** (adj.)   in-tr*uh*-**pur**-s*uh*-nl

Describing something which exists within a person.

<u>Intrapersonal</u> skills include things like time management and concentration which are under the control of the person concerned, cf. **interpersonal**.

<u>Progression words</u>
- intravenous
- intrapersonal

Vocabulary from Classical Roots

3. sub (L) "under", "less than", "beneath"

Core words
submerge
substandard
subordinate

xi) submerge (v) (I) s*uh*b-**murj**

The action of putting something under a liquid, usually water.

Modern nuclear submarines can stay submerged for weeks at a time.

xii) substandard (adj.) suhb-**stan**-derd

Describing something which is below a required level of quality.

Many countries have technical trade barriers designed to prevent substandard products, i.e. unsafe or fake items from entering the market.

xiii) subordinate (n) (c), (adj.) suh-**bawr**-dn-it

A person who is below another in rank in a hierarchy.

A secretary is subordinate to her boss and a soldier is subordinate to his commanding officer.

xiv) subconscious (adj.) suhb-**kon**-sh*uh* s

Describing something which exists in the mind beneath the level of consciousness.

Freud was one of the first psychologists to study the subconscious mind.

xv) subjunctive (n) (u) s*uh* b-**juhngk**-tiv

A mood of verb used in clauses which are doubtful, hypothetical, or grammatically subordinate to the main part of the sentence.

The subjunctive is one of the most difficult parts of English grammar for non-native speakers to learn.

Progression words
subconscious
subjunctive

4. supra (L)   "above"

Core words
superior
superb
supervise

xvi) **superior** (n) (c), (adj.)   suh-**peer**-ee-er

Someone who is of higher rank and has authority over others. / Something which is of higher quality than other products.

Companies often advertise their products as being of <u>superior</u> quality.

xvii) **superb** (adj.)   suh-**purb**

Describing something which is of the highest quality.

Rolls Royce have a reputation for making <u>superb</u> cars.

xviii) **supervise** (v) (T)   **soo**-per-vahyz

The action of checking and managing somebody else's work.

The ability to <u>supervise</u> staff effectively is a key management skill which employers look for.

xix) **supersonic** (adj.)   soo-per-**son**-ik

Describing something which moves at a speed above the speed of sound, i.e. 760mph at sea level.

The first man made object capable of <u>supersonic</u> travel was the German V2 rocket at the end of World War II.

xx) **superfluous** (adj.)   soo-**pur**-floo-*uh*s

Describing resources which are over and above what is required or needed.

Companies run lean manufacturing programmes in order to eliminate <u>superfluous</u> materials and labour during production.

Progression words
supersonic
superfluous

5. tele (G)   "far", "end", "remote"

Core words
- telescope
- telecommunications
- telecommuting

xxi) **telescope** (n) (c)   **tel**-*uh*-skohp

A scientific instrument for seeing things which are far Away, cf. microscope.

Telescopes can be used to observe the moon and stars.

xxii) **telecommunications** (n) (u)   tel-i-k*uh*-myoo-ni-**key**-sh*uh* nz

The process of communication over long distances using analogue or digital media.

The speed and data-carrying capacity of telecommunications have been transformed by information technology and the internet.

xxiii) **telecommuting** (n) (u)   **tel**-i-k*uh*-myoo-ting

The practice of working remotely and keeping in touch with colleagues via telephone, e-mail and video conferencing.

Telecommuting benefits the environment because it reduces the need for employees to commute to their offices every day.

xxiv) **telepathy** (n) (u)   t*uh*-**lep**-*uh*-thee

The ability to read another person's thoughts or feelings whilst being far away from them.

Belief in telepathy was widespread in the ancient world including among the Egyptians, Greeks and Romans.

xxv) **telemetry** (n) (u)   t*uh*-**lem**-i-tre

The practice of collecting data from a remote object for Analysis and monitoring.

Telemetry is essential for the development of driverless cars.

Progression words
- telepathy
- telemetry

Vocabulary from Classical Roots

6. trans (L)   "across", "beyond", "through"

xxvi) **transport** (v) (T), (n) (u)   trans-**pawrt**

Core words

transport

transnational

transparent

The action of moving goods or people from one place to another. / A collective noun for means of moving goods or people from one place to another

The search is on for means of <u>transport</u> which do not rely on fossil fuels.

xxvii) **transnational** (adj.)   trans-**nash**-uh-nl

Describing something which is across or beyond the borders of nations.

Some researchers argue that <u>transnational</u> companies are now more powerful than national governments.

xxviii) **transparent** (adj.)   trans-**pair**-*uh*nt

Describing a material which allows light to pass through it.

Ancient Roman women were often criticised for wearing <u>transparent</u> clothes.

xxix) **transcript** (n) (c)   **tran**-skript

A written record of something, usually originally spoken.

In the social sciences, qualitative researchers will often record oral interviews and then make a written <u>transcript</u> for analysis.

xxx) **transpose** (v) (T)   trans-**pohz**

To cause two or more items to exchange places.

Little kids sometimes <u>transpose</u> letters in a word.

Progression words

transcript

transpose

61

Vocabulary from Classical Roots

N.B.

Antonyms

Several words in this lesson have antonyms formed from by using a different root as a prefix. Complete the following diagram with words from the lesson. One additional opposite is given as an example:

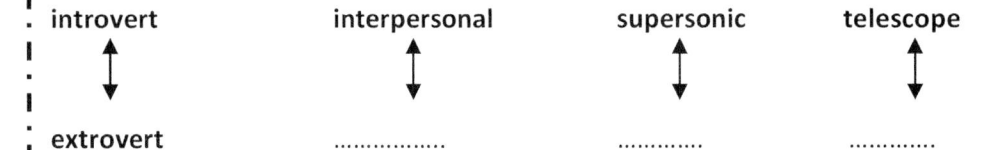

introvert	**interpersonal**	**supersonic**	**telescope**
↕	↕	↕	↕
extrovert	……………..	…………..	…………..

Making notes of relationships between words in this way helps you remember them.

Collocations

One way to learn collocations of adjectives and nouns is by using spider-grams:

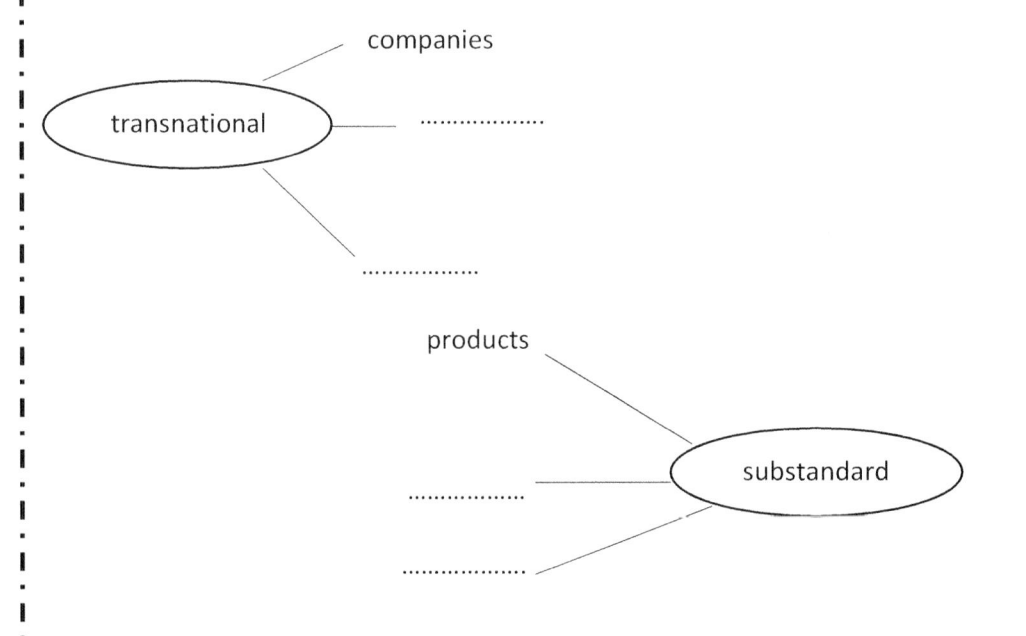

transnational — companies
transnational — ………………
transnational — ………………

substandard — products
substandard — ………………
substandard — ………………

Section B: Unit 3, Exercises

Exercise 1: Antonyms and collocations

Choose the best answer for each of the following questions:

1. (   ) Which of the following is an **antonym** of permanent?

    a) temporary   b) temporal   c) perennial   d) contemporary

2. (   ) Which one of the following **collocations** is incorrect?

    a) supersonic aircraft   b) transnational organisation

    c) predict the past   d) chronic disease

3. (   ) Which of the following is an **antonym** of preface?

    a) introduction   b) postscript   c) previous   d) chapter

4. (   ) Which one of the following is a correct word formed with the root tele?

    a) teledrome   b) telescreen   c) telenet   d) telemetry

5. (   ) Which of the following is an **antonym** of introvert?

    a) interview   b) introvert   c) extrovert   d) intermission

6. (   ) Which of the following is an **antonym** of ultra-modern?

    a) antediluvian   b) antecedent   c) contemporary   d) chronological

7. (   ) Which of the following **collocates** with intransitive?

    a) noun   b) grammar   c) adjective   d) verb

8. (   ) Which one of the following **collocations** is correct?

    a) transparent steel   b) asynchronous time   c) retro future   d) subordinate CEO

Exercise 2: Jumbled letters

Put the letters in the right order to make a word from this unit. The root is given to help you and the first one has been done for you as an example:

1. rlosuuppsef (super)   superfluous

2. tntnealaa   (ante)   ....

3. drpcetnee   (pre)   ....

4. gmltoucmtiene (tele)   ....

5. psrnatose (trans)   ....

6. isrttncoenei (inter)   ....

7. jvusbceiutn (sub)   ....

8. isnueovtran (intra)   ....

Vocabulary from Classical Roots

Exercise 3: Matching definitions

Match the word in box A with a definition from Box B.

	Box A		Box B
1.	subconscious	a)	An event which occurred before World War II, e.g. the Munich Agreement.
2.	anteroom	b)	To cause something, e.g. a meeting to happen at a later date or time.
3.	telepathy	c)	A small reception room where visitors wait to see the master of the house.
4.	postpone	d)	A short period of time between two parts of a performance in a theatre or cinema.
5.	intermission	e)	A feeling which occurs below the level of the conscious mind.
6.	transport	f)	Describing something to do with time.
7.	pre-war	g)	The ability to divine the thoughts of another person from a long distance.
8.	temporal	h)	The action of moving goods or people from one place to another, e.g. by road or rail.

1. ………   2. …….   3. …….   4. ………
5. ………   6. …….   7. …….   8. ………

Section B: Unit 4, Lesson A – Body Parts

1. phys (G), psych (G)   "the body"/ "nature", "the mind"

Core words

physics

physician

psychologist

---

i) **physics** (n) (u)   **fiz**-iks

The study of natural phenomena.

Physics is more popular among boys than girls in almost every country.

ii) **physician** (n) (c)   fi-**zish**-uh n

A person who is legally qualified to practice medicine.

The works of the ancient Greek physician Claudius Galen (131-200CE) had an enormous influence on the development of western medicine.

iii) **psychologist** (n) (c)   sahy-**kol**-uh-jist

A person who studies the human mind.

Sports psychologists help athletes understand and control their mental processes.

iv) **physique** (n) (u)   fi-**zeek**

The shape and structure of a person's body.

Young people today pay a lot of attention to their physique.

v) **psychometric** (adj.)   sahy-**kom**-i-trik

Describing something related to the properties of the mind or personality.

More and more employers use psychometric testing to select new employees to ensure that they will fit well with the existing staff.

Progression words

physique

psychometric

Vocabulary from Classical Roots

2. cardio (G)   "heart"

Core words
- cardiac
- cardiologist
- cardiology

vi) **cardiac** (adj.)   **kahr**-dee-ak

Describing something related to the heart.

Cardiac problems are becoming more common as people live longer.

vii) **cardiologist** (n) (c)   kahr-dee-**ol**-*uh*-jist

A doctor who specialises in treating heart diseases.

The South African cardiologist Dr Christian Barnard was the first surgeon to carry out a heart transplant.

viii) **cardiology** (n) (u)   kahr-dee-**ol**-*uh*-jee

The study of the heart, its diseases and treatments.

In many countries, cardiology is the most prestigious branch of medicine.

ix) **cardiovascular** system (n) (c)   kahr-dee-*uh*-**vas**-ky*uh*-ler **sis**-t*uh*m

The complete blood circulation system including the heart.

An athlete's cardiovascular efficiency controls their level of energy, stamina and speed of recovery from exertion.

x) **myocardium** (n) (u)   mahy-*uh*-**kahr**-dee-*uh*m

A layer of muscle which forms the main part of the heart wall.

Failure of the myocardium is one of the main causes of death from heart disease.

Progression words
- cardiovascular
- myocardium

3. derma (G), ortho (G), "skin", "straight"

Core words
dermatologist
dermatitis
orthodontics

xi) **dermatologist** (n) (c)   dur-m*uh*-**tol**-*uh*-jist

A doctor who specialises in treating skin conditions.

A person who has been burned by chemicals will need treatment from a <u>dermatologist</u>.

xii) **dermatitis** (n) (u)   dur-m*uh*-**tahy**-tis

Inflammation of the skin.

Symptoms of <u>dermatitis</u> include red and itchy skin.

xiii) **orthodontics** (n) (c)   awr-th*uh*-**don**-tiks

A branch of dentistry which straightens teeth.

<u>Orthodontics</u> uses braces to correct misshapen teeth and improve people's appearance.

xiv) **orthopaedic** (adj.)   or-tho-**pae**-dic

Describing something related to bones.

An <u>orthopaedic</u> surgeon fixes broken bones so that they are straight again.

xv) **pachyderm** (n) (c)   **pak**-i-durm

A class of animals with very thick skin.

Elephants are <u>pachyderms</u> and their thick skin protects them from both sharp objects, such as thorns, and bacteria.

Progression words
orthopaedic
pachyderm

Vocabulary from Classical Roots

4. manu (L), ped (L) "hand", "foot"

Core words
manual
pedestrian
manufacture

xvi) **manual** (adj.), (n) (c)   **man**-yoo-*uh* l   *

Describing something done by hand. / A book of instructions for how to use a machine.

<u>Manual</u> jobs are increasingly being replaced by robots. / Printed <u>manuals</u> for computers and mobile phones have increasingly been replaced by information on websites.

xvii) **pedestrian** (n) (c), (adj.)   p*uh*-**des**-tree-*uh* n

Someone who travels on foot. / Describing something which happens slowly; at the speed of a person walking.

<u>Pedestrians</u> are more likely to be injured in road accidents than car drivers. / Critics say that responses to the threat of climate change are proceeding at a <u>pedestrian</u> pace.

xviii) **manufacture** (v) (T)   man-y*uh*-**fak**-cher   *

The action of making something, usually in large quantities.

Toyota <u>manufacture</u> just under 9 million cars per year worldwide.

xix) **manuscript** (n) (c)   **man**-y*uh*-skript

A document written by hand.

Ancient Roman <u>manuscripts</u> were usually written on long rolls of parchment called scrolls, not on paper.

Scroll

xx) **pedicure** (n) (c)   **ped**-i-ky*oo* r

Professional care and treatment of the feet.

Regular <u>pedicure</u> is important for people who need to walk a lot.

Progression words
manuscript
pedicure

5. op/optis (G), or/oralis (L)   "eye"/ "sight" , "opening"/ "mouth"

Core words
- optician
- oral
- fibre-optic cable

xxi) **optician** (n) (c)   op-**tish**-*uh* n

A person who tests eyesight, makes and sells glasses.

A good <u>optician</u> can help short-sighted people see normally again.

xxii) **oral** (adj.)   **awr**-*uh* l

Describing something related to the mouth.

Most learners find <u>oral</u>, spoken Chinese more difficult than written Chinese.

xxiii) **fibre-optic cable** (n) (c)   **fahy**-ber-**op**-tik-**key**-b*uh* l

A type of cable used in digital communications made of tiny glass or plastic filaments that carry light beams.

<u>Fibre-optic cables</u> transmit broadband internet into your home and office.

xxiv) **orifice** (n) (c)   **awr**-*uh*-fis

A hole or opening in something.

The mouth, nostrils and ears are all <u>orifices</u> in the human body.

xxv) **autopsy** (n) (c)   **aw**-top-see

A visual examination of a body in order to find the cause of death.

The police will usually ask for an <u>autopsy</u> to be carried out if they find a body and are not sure if the person died as a result of a crime.

Progression words
- orifice
- autopsy

6. osteo (G), neur (G) "bone", "nerve"

xxvi) **osteopath** (n) (c)   **os**-tee-*uh*-path

A doctor who specialises in the treatment of bone disorders

Several sports stars have had their careers saved by an <u>osteopath</u> after damaging bones.

Core words

osteopath

neurotic

neuralgia

xxvii) **neurotic** (adj.)   ny*oo*-**rot**-ik

Describing someone suffering the mental illness, neurosis.

<u>Neurotic</u> people are suffering from excessive levels of anxiety and may exhibit symptoms such as jealousy, guilt and depression.

xxviii) **neuralgia** (n) (u)   n*oo*-**ral**-j*uh*

A medical condition in which the patient experiences pain along the length of a nerve.

Neurosis and the resulting <u>neuralgia</u> can be treated by **psychologists**.

xxix) **osteoporosis** (n) (u)   os-tee-oh-p*uh*-**roh**-sis

A medical condition in which bones become brittle and easily broken.

<u>Osteoporosis</u> is common among old people and means that they have to be careful to avoid falls.

xxx) **neurosurgeon** (n) (c)   n*oo* r-oh-**sur**-j*uh*-un

A doctor who carries out operations on the nervous system.

To become a <u>neurosurgeon</u> requires years of training and a very high level of skill.

Progression words

osteoporosis

neurosurgeon

N.B.

Roots and suffixes

We have seen that Greek and Latin roots often form the **prefix** of an English word. However, they can also be combined with **suffixes**, which are also of Greek and Latin origin, to make families of related words. These are usually academic words. In this lesson we have met three main types of words formed in this way. All of them are nouns.

People	Academic subjects	Medical conditions
physic<u>ian</u>	phys<u>ics</u>	dermat<u>itis</u>
psycholog<u>ist</u>	cardi<u>ology</u>	osteopor<u>osis</u>
cardiolog<u>ist</u>	orthodont<u>ics</u>	neural<u>gia</u>
dermatolog<u>ist</u>		
pedestr<u>ian</u>		
optic<u>ian</u>		
osteo<u>path</u>		
neurosurg<u>eon</u>		

There are no rules about which suffix is used with which root. Do not invent your own combinations. You just have to use a dictionary and learn them. However, classifying words by topic like this will help.

Chains of reasoning

xviii   **manufacture**

As discussed in Unit 2, some words have changed their meaning over the years but retained the same root. This is another example. Products that were once made by hand are now made by machines or robots but they are still made in large quantities in factories.

Section B: Unit 4, Lesson B – Age and Gender

1. pater (G)   "father"

    i) **paternal** (adj.)   p*uh*-**tur**-nl

> **Core words**
> paternal
> paternity
> patronage

    Describing something related to a father.

    Paternal behaviour includes a father assuming responsibility for his family.

    ii) **paternity leave** (n) (u)   p*uh*-**tur**-ni-tee leev

    A period of time off work granted to a father during and after the birth of his child.

    In some countries, such as Sweden, workers now have a legal right to paternity leave.

    iii) **patronage** (n) (u)   **pey**-tr*uh*-nij

    The power to grant money, jobs or political office in return for support.

    The power of patronage was traditionally held by men but this is changing as more and more women reach top positions in business and politics.

    iv) **patronising** (adj.)   **pey**-tr*uh*-nahyz-ing

    *Describing a situation in which one person considers themselves **superior** and looks down on another.*

    *Unfortunately, s*ome managers take a patronising attitude towards inexperienced **subordinates**.

    v) **patriarchal** (adj.)   pey-tree-**ahr**-k*uh* l

    Relating to a society controlled by men.

    In a patriarchal society, power and wealth are handed down from one generation to the next through the male line, i.e. sons.

> **Progression words**
> patronising
> patriarchal

Vocabulary from Classical Roots

2. mater (L)   "mother"

         vi) **maternal** (adj.)   m*uh*-**tur**-nl

> **Core words**
>
> maternal
>
> matrimony
>
> matrix

Describing something related to a mother.

It is generally believed that most women have <u>maternal</u> instincts to nurture children.

vii) **matrimony** (n) (u)   **ma**-tr*uh*-moh-nee   *

The state of being married.

The average age of <u>matrimony</u> is rising in most western countries.

viii) **matrix** (n) (c)   **mey**-triks   *

A network of interconnected objects or people originated from a common centre.

Modern large businesses are often structured like a <u>matrix</u>.

ix) **matriarchal** (adj.)   **mey**-tree-ahrk-ul

Relating to a society where a woman is the head.

There have been very few <u>matriarchal</u> societies in history in which power and wealth descended through the female line but the Naxi people of western China are an exception.

x) **matron** (n) (c)   **mey**-tr*uh* n

An old-fashioned word for a married woman who is mature, dignified and has authority.

In the past the head nurse in a hospital was often called the <u>matron</u> because of her age and position of authority.

> **Progression words**
>
> matron
>
> matriarchal

Vocabulary from Classical Roots

3. frater (L), soror (L), andr (G), gyno (G)   "brother", "sister", "man", "woman"

Core words
fraternal
fraternity
sorority

xi) **fraternal** (adj.)   fr*uh*-**tur**-nl

Describing something related to a brother or brothers.

In the 20th century it was common for socialists and trade unionists to send <u>fraternal</u> greetings to fellow members of the working class.

xii) **fraternity** (n) (c)   fr*uh*-**tur**-ni-tee

A social club with a male only membership.

<u>Fraternities</u> still play an important role in the social life of elite American universities.

xiii) **sorority** (n) (c)   s*uh*-**rawr**-i-tee

A social club with a female only membership.

<u>Sororities</u> still exist in some American universities but are less influential than their male equivalents.

xiv) **android** (n) (c)   **an**-droid

A machine in the form of a human being.

There are a lot of science fiction novels about <u>androids</u> trying to take over the world and they are usually assumed to have male powers.

xv) **androgynous** (adj.)   an-**droj**-*uh*-n*uh*s   *

Describing a person who has the physical appearance of neither a man nor a woman.

Known for being a tomboy as a child, she chose <u>androgynous</u> clothing instead of frilly dresses.

Progression words
android
androgynous

75

Vocabulary from Classical Roots

4. heter/hetero (G), homo (L), (G)   "different", "the same"

Core words
- heterogeneous
- homophone
- homogenous

xvi) **heterogeneous** (adj.)   het-er-*uh*-**seks**-yoo-*uh* l

Diverse in character or content.

The rich man had a large and <u>heterogeneous</u> collection of antiques from all parts of the world.

xvii) **homophone** (n) (c)   hoh-m*uh*-**seks**-yoo-*uh* l

Two words which have the same sound but different spellings or meanings.

Knight and night are <u>homophones.</u>

xviii) **homogeneous** (adj.)   h*uh*-**moj**-*uh*-n*uh* s

Describing a population of objects or living organisms which are all the same.

Scientific researchers like to use <u>homogeneous</u> populations in their experiments to eliminate as many variables as possible.

xix) **heterodox** (adj.)   **het**-er-*uh*-doks

Describing as person who holds opinions different from the norm, cf. orthodox.

Many religions punish people who hold <u>heterodox</u> beliefs.

xx) **homonym** (n) (c)   **hom**-*uh*-nim

Two words which have the same sound and spelling but different meanings.

English has only a few <u>homonyms</u> but Chinese has thousands.

Progression words
- heterodox
- homonym

5. paed (G), juven (L), ger (G)   "child", "young", "old age"

> **Core words**
> paediatric
> juvenile
> geriatric

xxi) **paediatric** (adj.)   pee-dee-**a**-triks

Describing a *branch of medicine specialising in the treatment of sick children.*

Great Ormond Street Hospital in London is a world centre of excellence in <u>paediatric</u> medicine.

xxii) **juvenile** (n) (c), (adj.)   **joo**-v*uh*-nl

A young person. / Describing something related to young people.

Peter cannot drive a car because he is still a <u>juvenile</u>. / <u>Juvenile</u> courts try young people accused of committing crimes.

xxiii) **geriatric** (adj.)   jer-ee-**a**-trik

Describing something related to old people.

As the population ages more and more people will need care in <u>geriatric</u> hospitals.

xxiv) **rejuvenate** (v)   ri-**joo**-v*uh*-neyt

To make somebody feel young again. / To revive something.

Tourism can <u>rejuvenate</u> the economy of decaying former industrial areas.

xxv) **paediatrician** (n) (c)   pee-dee-*uh*-**trish**-*uh*n

A doctor who specialises in the treatment of sick children.

More <u>paediatricians</u> are desperately needed in some of the world's poorest countries.

> **Progression words**
> rejuvenate
> paediatrician

Vocabulary from Classical Roots

6. nasc/nat (L), mort (L)   "birth", "death"

Core words
nativity
nascent
morbid

xxvi) **nativity** (n) (u), (adj.)   n*uh*-**tiv**-i-tee

Describing birth, usually of a human rather than an animal.

Many primary schools stage a nativity play every Christmas to celebrate the birth of Jesus.

xxvii) **nascent** (adj.)   nas-*uh* nt

Describing someone that is coming into being.

Rachel Carson was one of the leaders of the nascent environmental movement in the 1960s.

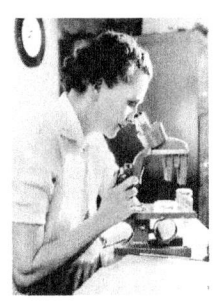

xxviii) **morbid** (adj.)   **mawr**-bid

Something gruesome, often related to disease or death.

Descriptions of death in Victorian novels often seem morbid to modern tastes.

xxix) **immortal** (adj.), (n) (c)   ih-**mawr**-tl

*Describing something which is **permanent** or never dies. / A person whose fame never dies.*

Isaac Newton's achievements were so great that his fame is immortal.

xxx) **mortality** (n) (u)   mawr-**tal**-i-tee

The condition of being dead.

The mortality rate is the number of people who die each year per thousand population.

Progression words
immortal
mortality

N.B.

Denotation and connotation

Denotation means the dictionary definition of a word. Connotation means the social and cultural associations the word has in every day speech. The problem, where roots are concerned, is that connotations can change over time. Many words connected with gender and age have different connotations today than they did when their roots were formed. For example, (v) patriarchal originally carried connotations of dignity and respect, but not anymore. Therefore, you need to be careful when using gender related root words to avoid giving offence.

Chains of reasoning

vii   **matrimony**

Until recently marriage defined the status and role of a woman much more than it did that of a man. Marriage was also believed to exist for the purpose of having children, hence the derivation of the word matrimony from the root, mater "mother".

viii   **matrix**

In ancient times a woman was seen as the centre of a network of family relationships as well as relationships in the community in her roles as daughter, mother, wife, cook, worker, etc., hence the derivation of the word matrix from the root mater "mother".

Section B: Unit 4, Exercises

Exercise 1: Matching roots and suffixes

Complete the spider-grams by matching roots and suffixes from this unit. The first one has been done for you as an example.

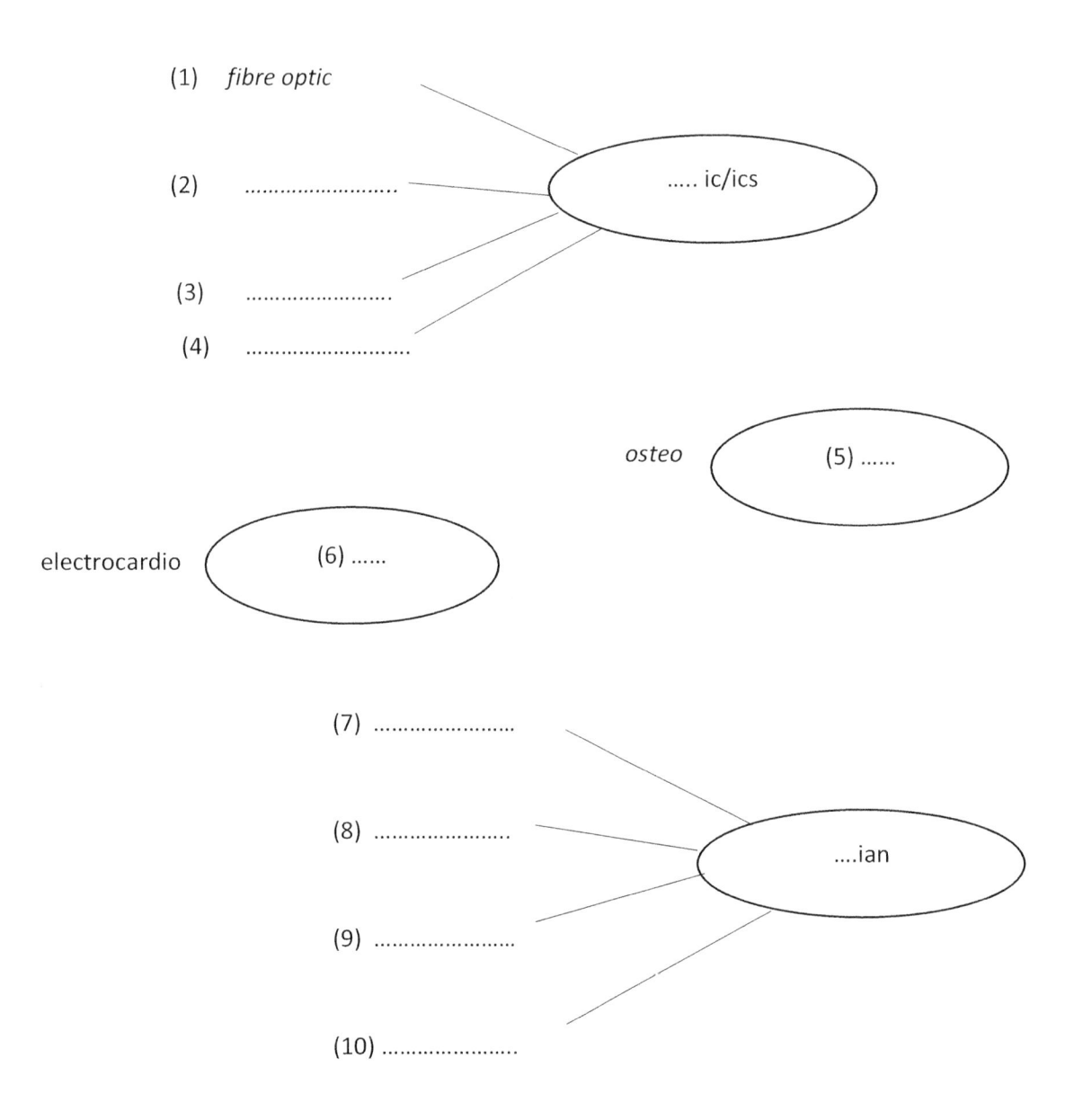

(1) *fibre optic*

(2) ....

(3) ....

(4) ....

..... ic/ics

osteo   (5) ......

electrocardio   (6) ......

(7) ....

(8) ....

(9) ....

(10) ....

....ian

Exercise 2: Fill in the Blanks

Complete the passage with the most appropriate words from the Word-bank. Each word can be used only once.

Word-bank

geriatric, mortality, paediatricians, natal, matrimony, juvenile, immortal, maternity, maternal

The stages of life are as old as human history, so it is not surprising that many of the words describing those stages derive from Greek and Latin roots. For most of us, before we were even born our mothers undergo (1) ante …………………….. care. Our mothers give birth in the (2) …………………….. ward of the local hospital. As infants we rely on the (3) …………………….. instincts of our mothers to look after us when we are too young to fend for ourselves. Modern children are luckier than their counterparts in ancient Greece or Rome. Nowadays most children grow up healthy but if they do become ill there are expert (4) …………………….. to treat them.

Things can get more difficult in our teenage years. The authorities, and many parents, worry about teenagers behaving badly. This is not new; the ancient Romans had the same fear of (5) …………………….. crime. Once we become adult, we all hope to fall in love and for most of us this leads to (6) …………………….. . Time moves on and we become parents then grandparents. Nowadays our life expectancy is much longer than the ancient Greeks or Romans and the (7) …………………….. rate is much lower. But eventually, in old age, many of us will need (8) …………………….. care in an old people's home or hospital. Finally, we must face the fact that none of us is (9) …………………….. but for a lucky few our achievements will live on after we die.

Exercise 3: Collocations

Match a word from column A with a word from column B to make collocations often used with root words. Hint: study the examples in this unit. The first one has been done for you as an example.

	Column A	Column B
1.	**paternity**	society
2.	fraternal	behaviour
3.	oral	greetings
4.	heterodox	movement
5.	pedestrian	job
6.	nascent	**leave**
7.	matriarchal	English
8.	manual	beliefs
9.	neurotic	pace

1. **paternity leave** 2. ……………………… 3. ………………………

4. ……………………… 5. ……………………… 6. ………………………

7. ……………………… 8. ……………………… 9. ………………………

Section B: Unit 5, Lesson A – Opinions

1. ab/av (L)   "away from"

i) **abhorrent** (adj.)   ab-**hor**-uhnt

Something that is wrong/unacceptable. / Shuddering away from in horror.

Most people, nowadays, find slavery <u>abhorrent</u>.

Core words

abhorrent

abnormal

aversion

---

ii) **abnormal** (adj.)   ab-**nawr**-m*uh*l

Describing something which deviates from accepted standards.

Most cultures define themselves by classifying behaviours and art forms as normal or <u>abnormal</u>.

iii) **aversion** (n) (c)   *uh*-**vur**-sh*uh*n

Having a feeling of strong opposition to an idea. / Having a strong dislike of something.

I have a strong <u>aversion</u> to the smell and taste of durian fruit.

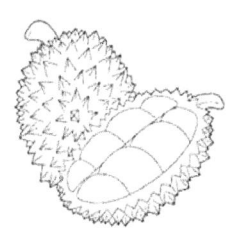

iv) **abstain** (v) (T), (I)   ab-**steyn**

To refrain from expressing an opinion. / To refuse to vote for or against something.

Several Senators <u>abstained</u> in yesterday's vote on the government's economic policies.

v) **aberration** (n) (c)   ab-*uh*-**rey**-sh*uh*n

An exception to normal standards of behaviour or performance, usually with negative connotations.

When accused of human rights abuses, the company claimed it was an <u>aberration</u> by one rogue supplier.

Progression words

abstain

aberration

---

2. anti (G) "against"

Core words
- antics
- antisocial
- antipathy

vi) **antics** (n) (u)   **an**-tiks

Behaviour which is silly, funny or against reason.

In some countries the general public are losing patience with what they see as the <u>antics</u> of politicians.

vii) **antisocial** (adj.)   an-tee-**soh**-sh*uh*l

Behaviour which makes it difficult for a person to make friends. / Behaviour which is defined as being against the interests of society.

<u>Antisocial</u> behaviour by **juveniles** has become a serious problem in some areas.

viii) **antipathy** (n) (c)   an-**tip**-*uh*-thee

A strong feeling of dislike towards somebody or something.

<u>Antipathy</u> is a synonym for **aversion** so I can also say I have an antipathy towards durian fruit.

ix) **antagonist** (n) (c)   an-**tag**-*uh*-nist

A person or persons you oppose or fight against.

The city states of Athens and Sparta were often <u>antagonists</u> in ancient Greece.

x) **antidote** (n) (c)   **an**-ti-doht

A medicine that counteracts a specific poison.

There is no known <u>antidote</u> to the poison of certain jellyfish.

Progression words
- antagonist
- antidote

3. contra/contro (L) "against"

Core words
- contrast
- contradict
- controversy

xi) contrast (n) (c), (v) (T)   **kon**-trast

The difference between two opposite items. / To show the difference between two items or ideas.

Students were asked to write an essay about the <u>contrasts</u> between realist and abstract art. / The professor <u>contrasted</u> capitalist and communist models of the economy in his lecture.

xii) contradict (v) (T)   kon-tr*uh*-**dikt**

To say that the truth is the opposite of somebody else's opinion.

Football fans often <u>contradict</u> each other about which team is the best.

xiii) controversy (n) (c)   **kon**-tr*uh*-vur-see

A public debate or argument about an issue usually involving many people over a long period.

There is a lot of <u>controversy</u> about climate change and how to respond to it.

xiv) contravene (v) (T)   kon-tr*uh*-**veen**

To act against a law or regulation.

Most people <u>contravene</u> traffic laws from time to time by speeding or parking in prohibited places.

xv) contretemps (n) (c)   **kon**-tr*uh*-tahn

An embarrassing incident which is against accepted rules of behaviour.

The movie star caused a <u>contretemps</u> by swearing during a live TV interview.

Progression words
- contravene
- contretemps

4. con (L)   "with", "together"

Core words
- connect
- connector
- concur

xvi) **connect** (v) (T)   k*uh*-**nekt**

To join together.

In persuasive writing it is important to <u>connect</u> your ideas together logically to make your opinions credible.

xvii) **connector** (n) (c)   k*uh*-**nek**-ter

Something that links two things together.

Correct use of a range of <u>connectors</u> including prepositions, demonstratives and relative clauses is one of the keys to expressing your opinions clearly and precisely.

xviii) **concur** (v) (T)   k*uh* n-**kur**

To agree with somebody else's opinion.

The Appeal Court Judges <u>concurred</u> with the decision of the lower court and found the defendant guilty.

xix) **connote** (v) (I) (T)   k*uh*-**noht**

To attach additional meaning to something.

In most countries owning designer label clothes <u>connotes</u> wealth and sophistication.

xx) **connotation** (n) (c)   kon-*uh*-**tey**-sh*uh*n

The meanings associated with a word in addition to its dictionary definition.

Many words, particularly adjectives, have cultural <u>connotations</u> and academic writers can choose such words to subtly express personal opinions without using non-academic expressions such as "I think".

Progression words
- connote
- connotation

5. pro (L)   "forward", "worthy"

Core words
- propose
- proposition
- approve

xxi) **propose** (v) (I) (T)   pr*uh*-**pohz**

To make a suggestion. / To ask a person to marry you.

He <u>proposed</u> on bended knee during a candlelit dinner in true romantic fashion.

xxii) **proposition** (n) (c)   prop-*uh*-**zish**-*uh* n

An idea which the proposer wishes others to accept.

In ancient Rome it was necessary to put forward a formal <u>proposition</u> in the Senate to enact a new law.

xxiii) **approve** (v) (T)   *uh*-**proov**

To have a favourable opinion of something. / To allow a proposed new law to pass.

In a recent opinion poll, most people <u>approved</u> of tougher laws against smoking.

xxiv) **proponent** (n) (c)   pr*uh*-**poh**-n*uh*nt

*A person who puts forward, or supports a **proposition**, cf. opponent.*

<u>Proponents</u> of carbon taxes claim they will act as an incentive to reduce emissions.

xxv) **probe** (v) (T), (n) (c)   prohb   *

To investigate something deeply to find the best solution. / An inquiry or instrument used to investigate deeply.

Investigative journalists <u>probe</u> deeply to uncover hidden and complex stories.

Progression words
- proponent
- probe

6. ob/op (L)   "against"

Core words
- oppose
- object
- obstruct

xxvi) **oppose** (v)   *uh*-**pohz**

To take action against something.

Animal rights activists <u>oppose</u> the use of animals for testing medicines or cosmetics.

xxvii) **object** (v) (T)   *uh*b-**jekt**

*To make a statement or gesture against a **proposition**.*

In California voters can <u>object</u> to a **proposition** by voting against it in a referendum.

xxviii) **obstruct** (v) (T)   *uh*b-**struhkt**

To make it difficult for somebody to take action or get a suggestion accepted.

Helping a criminal to <u>obstruct</u> justice, e.g. by providing a false alibi is a serious crime.

xxix) **opposition** (n) (u)   op-*uh*-**zish**-*uh*n

The expression of disagreement. / Organised groups of people working together to defeat an idea or proposal.

Plans to build new airports often arouse strong <u>opposition</u> from environmental campaigners.

xxx) **obdurate** (adj.)   **ob**-dy*oo*-rit

Describing someone who persists in their opinions or beliefs over a long period of time despite efforts to persuade them otherwise.

Medieval astronomers were <u>obdurate</u> in their belief that the sun orbited around the earth.

Progression words
- opposition
- obdurate

N.B.

Learning roots as prefixes

In previous units we have looked at spider-grams as a way of helping you remember new words. Another method that works equally well with roots used as prefixes is word dominoes.

Make yourself a set with a root prefix in the right-hand end of each domino and the remainder of a different word in the left-hand end. Try to match up as many as you can to make a chain.

Chains of reasoning

xxv   **probe**

Before Foucault and post-modernist philosophy, investigating something deeply, probing, in order to establish the truth was generally regarded as a good thing and a worthy use of time, hence the derivation of the word from a root meaning good or positive.

Vocabulary from Classical Roots

Section B: Unit 5, Lesson B – Positive and Negative

1. bene (L)   "good", "well"

Core words
- benefit
- beneficial
- benign

i) **benefit** (v), (n) (c)   ben-*uh*-fit

Something good or advantageous. / A social security payment.

In most western countries the unemployed receive state <u>benefits</u> to help them through their time of difficulty.

ii) **beneficial** (adj.)   ben-*uh*-**fish**-*uh*l

Describing something positive, good or helpful.

Private tutoring can be <u>beneficial</u> for student's exam scores.

iii) **benign** (adj.)   bih-**nahyn**

Describing something which is kind, gentle or favourable. / Not harmful.

The weather is really <u>benign</u> today, perfect for a day out in the countryside.

iv) **benevolent** (adj.)   b*uh*-**nev**-*uh*-l*uh*nt

Describing someone who has good intentions. / Describing an entity run to help people rather than make profits.

Peisistratos was a <u>benevolent</u> dictator in Athens during the sixth century BCE.

v) **benefactor** (n) (c)   ben-*uh*-fak-ter

A person who gives money for good causes.

Lord Wolfson was a generous <u>benefactor</u> to universities around the world.

Progression words
- benevolent
- benefactor

90

Vocabulary from Classical Roots

2. dis/dys (G) "badly", "ill", "abnormal"

Core words

dysfunctional

dyspepsia

dyslexia

vi) **dysfunctional** (adj.)   dis-**fuhngk**-sh*uh*-nl

Describing a system or organisation which is not working as intended.

After World War II the government of Germany was completely dysfunctional.

vii) **dyspepsia** (n) (u)   dis-**pep**-see-*uh*

A medical condition when food is badly digested.

Dyspepsia is popularly known as indigestion.

viii) **dyslexia** (n (u)   dis-**lek**-see-*uh*

A medical condition affecting the brain which makes it difficult to read and write.

Prejudice against students with dyslexia has gradually been reduced in recent years.

ix) **dystopia** (n) (u)   dis-**toh**-pee-*uh*

An imaginary world in which everything is bad, cf. utopia.

George Orwell's novel, 1984, is one of the most famous dystopias in fiction.

x) **dysentery** (n) (u)   **dis**-*uh* n-ter-ee

A bowel disease caused by drinking contaminated water.

Dysentery is treatable nowadays but nevertheless remains a major killer in developing countries.

Progression words

dystopia

dysentery

3. il, im (L)   "not", "without"

Core words
- illicit
- illegible
- immobile

xi) **illicit** (adj.)   ih-**lis**-it

Describing an activity or product which is not permitted or licensed.

During the 1920s alcohol was prohibited in the United States but illicit brewing and selling continued, often run by gangsters such as Al Capone.

xii) **illegible** (adj.)   ih-**lej**-*uh*-b*uh* l

Describing something which cannot be read.

The advent of e-mail means that having illegible handwriting is less of a handicap than it used to be.

xiii) **immobile** (adj.)   ih-**moh**-b*uh* l, - bahyl

Describing something which is static or cannot be moved, cf. mobile

The western front in World War I was a classic example of immobile warfare.

xiv) **impair** (v) (T)   im-**pair**

To reduce the performance, value or quality of something.

Some people believe that watching too much television impairs young children's development of speech and social skills.

xv) **implausible** (adj.)   im-**plaw**-z*uh*-b*uh*l

Describing something which does not seem believable.

Expert reviewers say that the blogger's claim to have found a cure for the common cold appears to be implausible.

Progression words
- impair
- implausible

4. in, ir (L)   "not", "without"

Core words
- inept
- irresponsible
- irrational

xvi) **inept** (adj.)   ih-**nept**

Describing a person or action that is without skill or competence.

Critics described the minister's speech in parliament as inept.

xvii) **irresponsible** (adj.)   ir-i-**spon**-s*uh*-b*uh*l

Describing something done in a reckless manner.

The judge said that the fairground owners had been irresponsible by allowing a dangerous ride to remain in operation.

xviii) **irrational** (adj.)   ih-**rash**-*uh*-nl

Describing a belief or action which is not based on reason, facts or evidence.

Belief in ghosts is usually regarded as irrational.

xix) **inadmissible** (adj.)   in-*uh* d-**mis**-*uh*-b*uh* l

In law, describing evidence which cannot be used in a trial.

Confessions obtained by torture are inadmissible in most courts.

xx) **irresistible** (adj.)   ir-i-**zis**-t*uh*-b*uh* l

Describing feelings which are so strong that they overcome self-control.

Lucy found chocolate to be an irresistible temptation even though she was trying to diet.

Progression words
- inadmissible
- irresistible

5. neg (L)   "deny"

Core words
- negate
- renege
- renegade

xxi) **negate** (v) (T)   **neg**-eyt

The action of making something ineffective.

The recent hurricane <u>negated</u> all the progress made in improving the island's infrastructure over the last **decade**.

xxii) **renege** (v)   ri-**neg**

To go back on an agreement or promise.

The company are suing their supplier for <u>reneging</u> on a commitment not to raise prices.

xxv) **negativity** (n) (u)   **neg**-*uh*-tiv-ity

The tendency to hold a negative opinion about all or most things.

Consultants found that there was a lot of <u>negativity</u> among employees after years of static salaries and job losses.

xxiii) **renegade** (n) (c)   **ren**-i-geyd

A person who deserts a country, political party or cause for another.

A footballer who signs for a rival team is often regarded as a <u>renegade</u> by his former fans.

xxiv) **abnegate** (v)   **neg**-*uh*-tiv **kur**-*uh*nt

Renounce or reject something.

He decided to <u>abnegate</u> unhealthy eating in order to be fit.

Progression words
- renegade
- abnegate

6. prob/prov (L)   "prove"

Core words
- probability
- reprove
- probation

xxvi) **probability** (n) (u)   prob-*uh*-**bil**-i-tee

In general use, the chance of something happening. / In math, an expression to show the likelihood of an event occurring.

Nearly all models of risk in business and finance are based on the mathematical theory of probability.

xxvii) **reprove** (v) (T)   ri-**proov**

To criticise, or correct somebody's behaviour, usually in a mild way.

The teacher reproved her students for not paying attention in class.

xxviii) **probation** (n) (u)   proh-**bey**-sh*uh* n

The grant of a right or position dependent on conditions or performance.

In some countries a young teacher is given a job on probation for a year while his/her performance is assessed.

xxix) **approbation** (n) (u)   ap-r*uh*-**bey**-sh*uh* n

An expression of approval.

The award of a medal by a government is a mark of approbation of a person's contribution to society.

xxx) **probate** (n) (c)   **proh**-beyt

The official proving of a will.

He was granted a probate to execute her grandmother's estate.

Progression words
- approbation
- probate

95

N.B.

Register

Register means the degree of formality of a word and therefore the context in which it is used. Register is usually classified as **formal (F)** or **informal (I)**.

The vast majority of words based on Greek and Latin roots are formal. There are sometimes, but not always, equivalent informal, idiomatic or slang words or expressions.

Example

xxvii)   reprove (v) formal

tell off (phrasal verb) informal

Formal words based on Greek or Latin roots are very useful for academic study or formal business or legal writing but sound strange in everyday speech. For native speakers of English which register to use is usually instinctive. But non-native speakers learning English as a foreign language often need help. Some students often use formal words inappropriately in everyday situations in a misguided attempt to prove their fluency.

Study Tip

If you are unsure about register mark new words in your notebook, e.g.

vi) dysfunctional (adj.) (F)

useless (adj.) (I)

Section B: Unit 5, Exercises

Exercise 1: Matching root prefixes and endings

Match the endings in the Word-bank with the prefix headings in the table below to make correct words. There is only one possible answer. The first one has been done for you as an example.

ab	anti	bene	contra	im	prob
abstain					

Word-bank

….**stain**	….pathy	…..dote	…..normal
….vene	…..dict	…..factor	…..ficial
…..mobile	…..plausible	…..ability	…..ation

Exercise 2: Multiple choice: Collocations and register

Choose the best option to complete each of the following sentences:

1. (   ) If an organisation is dysfunctional, a less formal way to describe it would be .... :

    a) excellent   b) useless   c) silly   d) illegal

2. (   ) Which of the following nouns often collocates with the adjective temptation?

    a) speech   b) disease   c) irresistible   d) handwriting

3. *(   )* George Orwell's novel 1984 is a warning about a possible future .... Which of the following words best completes this sentence?

    a) dystopia   b) negativity   c) dyspepsia   d) probability

4. (   ) Which formal word derived from a root meaning "worthy" or "good" is a synonym for the verb to tell off?

    a) renege   b) approbation   c) irresponsible   d) reprove

5. (   ) Proponents are people who .... an idea or policy.

    a) oppose   b) go back on   c) put forward   d) abstain

6. (   ) A formal, academic word meaning to agree with is

    a) connector   b) connotation   c) concur   d) connote

7. (   ) The informal word *kind* is a synonym for which of the following formal words?

    a) aversion   b) benign   c) negate   d) antipathy

8. (   ) Which of the following is it easy to contravene?

    a) evidence   b) judgement   c) opposition   d) laws

Vocabulary from Classical Roots

Exercise 3: Word search

Note: One word (PROBE) has been done for you as an example.

G	B	E	G	A	I	H	A	I	C	D	U	R	K	A
B	T	Z	H	M	B	W	T	V	F	F	U	E	R	N
Y	I	N	P	P	C	E	J	D	L	B	F	N	M	T
V	V	A	E	J	G	D	R	E	T	W	G	E	E	A
Z	I	U	V	L	Q	A	L	R	P	J	D	G	M	G
R	U	I	A	Y	O	E	C	K	A	E	M	A	Y	O
T	O	L	F	W	K	V	G	O	T	T	U	D	T	N
C	O	N	T	R	E	T	E	M	P	S	I	E	U	I
Q	V	O	H	P	S	U	F	N	F	Y	R	O	I	S
H	K	K	C	V	G	R	T	L	E	Z	B	C	N	T
C	Y	F	M	E	L	Q	M	M	U	B	O	W	D	L
E	T	A	C	I	D	U	J	D	A	D	R	L	T	Z
D	Y	S	P	E	P	S	I	A	Y	F	P	O	Q	X
U	K	P	R	O	Z	E	B	O	R	P	P	J	F	S
R	H	U	K	P	N	C	P	X	J	S	O	Q	D	N

ABERRATION   ADJUDICATE   ANTAGONIST
BENEVOLENT   CONTRETEMPS   DYSPEPSIA
IMPAIR   PROBE
RENEGADE

Consolidation 1 – Units 1-5

Activity A.   **Building your own Word-bank**

As we have learned in Units 1-5, many of the words formed from Greek and Latin roots are members of word families. In this exercise we are going to use dictionaries to complete a table and add to the families of some of the words we have learned. This is a technique you can then use independently to increase your vocabulary further. Remember:

i) There are standard suffixes which tell you the part of speech of a word

Verb	Noun	Adjective
……. ise	…….. age	…… able
	…… ment	……. ics
	……. tion	…… ial
	……. ics	….. ory
	…….. ist	…… ent
		…… ed
		…… ing

Use these suffixes to help you complete the table but remember there are no rules about which suffix matches which root. Check your dictionary.

ii) Not all word families contain every part of speech.
iii) Some families contain more than one noun. Typically, one will be a person and the other an object, a statement or an academic subject.

iv) Some families contain more than one adjective, typically ending in ….*ed* for a state of a mind and ….*ing* for an object or process.

v) Many families have negative verbs, nouns and adjectives formed by adding root prefixes such as those we learned in Unit 5.

vi) Some families also have adverbs but we will deal with these in Unit 6.

Words taught in Units 1-5 are shown in bold.

Verb	Noun (s)	Adjective (s)
predict	a) *object*: b) *agent*:	a) *positive*: b) *negative*:
supervise		
	telescope	
xxxxxxxxxxxxxxxx	a) *subject*: b) *person*: **psychologist**	
manufacture		a) *state*: b) *process*:
	a) *person*: b) *practice*: **patronage**	a) *condition*: b) *behaviour*: **patronising**

contradict		
	connector	a) *positive:* b) *negative:* **badly connected**
a) *positive:* **approve** b) *negative:*	a) *positive:* b) *negative:*	a) *state of mind:* b) *condition:*
a) *positive:* b) *negative:*	a) *person:* b) *opinion:* **opposition**	

Activity B: Writing

Write a description of a person or an organisation you are familiar with. Use as many adjectives as you can from Units 1-5. You should write at least 250 words.

Section B: Unit 6, Lesson A – The Five Senses

1. aud (L)   "hearing", "sound"

Core words
- audible
- audience
- audiovisual

i) **audible** (adj.)   aw-d*uh*-buh l

Describing something which can be heard, cf. inaudible.

Residents complain that traffic from the nearby motorway is audible all the time.

ii) **audience** (n) (c)   aw-dee-*uh* ns

A group of people listening to or watching a performance of some kind.

With the arrival of 3D sound and vision, cinema audiences have increased substantially.

iii) **audiovisual** (adj.)   aw-dee-oh-**vizh**-oo-*uh* l

Describing something that communicates via a combination of sound and vision.

Teachers often use audio-visual aids to make classes more interesting.

iv) **audition** (n) (c), (v)   aw-**dish**-*uh* n

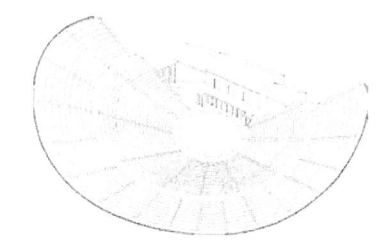

A test for actors and models to decide who to cast in a role. / To take part in a test to choose someone for a role.

Auditions were important in ancient Greek theatre because in the days before PA systems the quality of an actor's voice was crucial.

v) **auditorium** (n) (c)   aw-di-**tohr**-ee-*uh* m

A large room designed for listening to a performance.

The auditorium of Sydney Opera house is famous for the quality of its acoustics.

Progression words
- audition
- auditorium

Vocabulary from Classical Roots

2. phon (G)   "sound"

Core words
- microphone
- symphony
- cacophony

vi) microphone (n) (c)   **mahy**-kr*uh*-fohn

An electrical device used to amplify and transmit sound.

Several people including David Hughes and Thomas Edison claimed to have invented the <u>microphone</u>.

vii) symphony (n) (c),   **sim**-f*uh*-nee

A piece of classical music which combines the sounds of a large number of instruments.

Ludwig van Beethoven (1712-1773) wrote nine <u>symphonies</u>.

viii) cacophony (n) (c)   k*uh*-**kof**-*uh*-nee

A lot of competing noises, or voices combining to make an unpleasant noise.

The street markets of ancient Rome must have been a <u>cacophony</u> as rival vendors shouted about their goods.

ix) phonics (n) (u)   **fon**-iks

A method of teaching vocabulary based on the sounds of words rather than their spelling.

<u>Phonics</u> are used in this book to help students pronounce new words.

x) phonology (n) (u)   f*uh*-**nol**-*uh*-jee

The study of the sounds and pronunciation of a language.

<u>Phonology</u> was very important in helping 19th century European explorers and missionaries develop written scripts for African and Asian languages which previously had been only spoken.

Progression words
- phonics
- phonology

3. tact/tag/tang (L)   "touch", "feel"

Core words
contact
intact
tactile

xi) **contact** (v) (T), (n) c)   **kon**-takt

The act of touching something. / The action of communicating with another person. / A person you network with in business.

The meaning of contact has changed since ancient Greece and Rome because digital technology now allows people to make **asynchronous** contact with each other.

xii) **intact** (adj.)   in-**takt**   *

Describing something which is whole, in one piece and not broken.

The Romans fought for centuries to keep their empire intact in the face of barbarian invasions.

xiii) **tactile** (adj.)   **tak**-tahyl

Describing a person who likes touching something.

Some students are tactile learners who acquire knowledge by touching real objects rather than reading about them.

xiv) **contagious** (adj.)   k*uh* n-**tey**-j*uh* s

Describing something which is passed from one person to another by direct contact.

Control of contagious diseases such as Ebola is a major public health challenge.

xv) **tangible** (adj.)   **tan**-j*uh*-b*uh*l

Describing something which can be touched.

Archaeology provides tangible evidence of what life was like in ancient Greece and Rome.

Progression words
contagious
tangible

4. vid, vis (L) "see" "sight"

Core words
- visual
- video
- visibility

xvi) **visual** (adj.) **vizh**-oo-*uh* l

Describing something relating to sight.

Many shoppers choose clothes based on their visual impression of the product.

xvii) **video** (n) (c), (u) **vid**-ee-oh

Content containing moving images intended to be watched.

Video sharing platforms such as YouTube have transformed the way young people watch movies and sport.

xviii) **visibility** (n) (u) viz-*uh*-**bil**-i-tee

The state of being visible. / The degree to which something is visible.

Poor visibility due to fog is a major cause of road accidents.

xix) **vista** (n) (c) **vis**-t*uh*

A view over a wide area.

The London Eye provides spectacular vistas across the city for tourists.

xx) **visage** (n) (c) **viz**-ij

A person's face or appearance.

Models are expected to present an attractive visage to the camera.

Progression words
- vista
- visage

5. odour (L)   "smell"

Core words
odour
deodorant
odourless

xxi) odour (n) (c)   **oh**-der

The smell of something.

Many animals, such as skunks, have a distinctive <u>odour</u> which they use to attract prey or repel enemies.

xxii) deodorant (n) (c)   dee-**oh**-der-*uh* nt

A chemical used to destroy unpleasant smells.

Modern aerosol <u>deodorants</u> were first introduced by Gillette in the early 1960s.

xxiii) odourless (adj.)   **oh**-der-les

The property of not having a smell.

One of the reasons that Carbon Monoxide is so dangerous is that it is <u>odourless</u>.

xxiv) malodorous (adj.)   mal-**oh**-der-*uh* s

Describing something which has a very bad smell.

When I was a boy it was a popular schoolboy prank to release "stink bombs" made of hydrogen sulphide in the classroom because it is <u>malodorous</u> and would annoy the teacher.

xxv) odoriferous (adj.)   oh-d*uh*-**rif**-er-*uh*s

Describing something which gives off a smell.

The human body is <u>odoriferous</u> unless washed frequently.

Progression words
malodorous
odoriferous

6. voc/voci (L)   "voice", "call"

Core words
- vocal
- vocabulary
- advocate

xxvi) **vocal** (adj.), (n) (u)   **voh**-k*uh*l

Describing something related to the voice. / Singing the words of a song.

I love the <u>vocals</u> in Whitney Houston's albums.

xxvii) **vocabulary** (n) (u)   voh-**kab**-y*uh*-ler-ee

The range of words and expressions a person is able to use in speech and/or writing.

Some experts believe that watching too much television or too many videos on YouTube **impairs** young children's development of <u>vocabulary</u>.

xxviii) **advocate** (v) (T), (n) (c)   (*v*) **ad**-v*uh*-keyt; (n) **ad**-v*uh*-kit

To propose or support an idea or policy. / A lawyer who speaks on somebody's behalf in court.

Some environmentalists <u>advocate</u> a carbon tax to force industry to take responsibility for the pollution it causes.

xxix) **vocalize** (v) (T) (I)   **voh**-k*uh*-lahyz

The action of producing speech.

The movie "The King's Speech" showed that people who stammer have difficulty in <u>vocalizing</u> clearly but they can be helped.

xxx) **vociferous** (adj.)   voh-**sif**-er-*uh*s

Talking about something in a loud or persistent manner.

In many countries there has been <u>vociferous</u> **opposition** to war.

Progression words
- vocalize
- vociferous

N.B.

Study Skills: Writing your own examples

Every word in this book is accompanied by an example of the word used in a sentence.

But you will learn even more by writing your own additional example sentences.

Steps:

i) Check the part of speech, e.g. noun, verb. Use the new word with the same function in your sentence.

ii) Think about the topic. Some words can be used in a wide range of contexts, e.g. (xi) contact. Others are topic specific, e.g. terms in math, law or medicine. So, think about a suitable topic.

iii) Try to come up with a sentence related to your high school or college studies. This will help you develop vocabulary you can use to improve your assignment scores.

iv) If possible, have your example sentences checked by a teacher for grammar and spelling.

Chains of reasoning

(xii) The word **intact** came from the Latin verb *intactus* which had **connotations** of something being undefiled, uninjured as well as being in one piece. But like many root words its meaning and usage has widened over the years as the cultural importance of the original meaning has diminished.

Section B: Unit 6, Lesson B – Feelings

1. ami/amo (L)   "love", "liking"

Core words
- amity
- amicably
- amenity

i) **amity** (n) (u)   **am**-i-tee

A state of friendship and harmony.

There has never been amity between the nations of the Middle East.

ii) **amicably** (adv.)   **am**-i-k*uh*-b*uh*l

Describing a manner of doing something characterised by friendship and goodwill.

The directors of both companies agreed amicably to merge their operations.

iii) **amenity** (n) (c)   *uh*-**men**-i-tee

A facility where people can meet to take part in social activities.

The local council have promised to build more amenities such as a leisure centre and a park.

iv) **enamour** (v) (T)   ih-**nam**-er

To charm or captivate someone. / To make someone enthusiastic about an idea.

Elon Musk is enamoured with the idea of building human colonies on other planets.

v) **amorously** (adv.)   **am**-er-*uhs*-lee

Describing something done in a manner suggestive of romance, or love.

Numerous figures in the entertainment industry have recently got into trouble for behaving amorously towards young performers or staff.

Progression words
- enamour
- amorously

Vocabulary from Classical Roots

2. ego (L), (G)   "self"

Core words
- ego
- egotistical
- ego trip

vi) **ego** (n) (c)   **ee**-goh

A person's sense of self and personal identity.

A lot of celebrities are accused of having a big <u>ego</u>.

vii) **egotistical** (adj.)   ee-g*uh*-**tis**-ti-k*uh* l

Describing someone who is vain, selfish or opinionated.

Someone who is <u>egotistical</u> is unlikely to have many long-term friends.

viii) **ego trip** (n (c)   **ee**-goh-trip

An experience intended to satisfy personal desires without regard to others.

My brother's talk about becoming a Premier League footballer is just an <u>ego trip</u> because he doesn't have any talent.

ix) **alter ego** (n) (c)   **awl**-ter **ee**-goh

A person who is very like yourself; another side of one's personality.

The pop singer David Bowie created the character, Ziggy Stardust to be his <u>alter ego</u>.

x) **egocentric** (adj.)   ee-goh-**sen**-trik

Describing a personality in which the self is dominant.

<u>Egocentric</u> CEOs ignore the interests of other stakeholders such as employees, customers and the environment.

Progression words
- alter ego
- egocentric

3. path (G) "feeling", "disease"

Core words
- apathy
- empathy
- sympathetically

xi) **apathy** (n) (u)   ap-*uh*-thee

The state of not caring about a particular situation or about things in general.

Many young people show complete <u>apathy</u> towards politics.

xii) **empathy** (n) (u)   **em**-p*uh*-thee

The state of being able to understand the situation and feelings of others.

Successful business leaders have strong <u>empathy</u> with their customers and employees.

xiii) **sympathetically** (adv.)   sim-p*uh*-**thet**-ikali

Describing a manner of doing something which shows care and compassion for the troubles of others.

Aid workers listened <u>sympathetically</u> to the stories of refugees fleeing from the country's civil war.

xiv) **pathetic** (adj.)   p*uh*-**thet**-ik

Describing a performance which attempts to move the emotions by self-abasement. / A very poor performance.

The minister was sacked after his performance in his latest TV interview was described as <u>pathetic</u> on social media.

xv) **homeopathy** (n) (u)   hoh-mee-**op**-*uh*-thee

A holistic medical treatment which uses very small amounts of the substance that caused the condition.

<u>Homeopathy</u> is popular among those who fear the power and side effects of modern drugs.

Progression words
- pathetic
- homeopathy

4. phil (G)   "love", "friendship"

> **Core words**
>
> philosophy
>
> philanthropist
>
> philistine

xvi) **philosophy** (n) (u)   fi-**los**-*uh*-fee

The study of the rational principles of truth, knowledge and ethics./ An approach to life.

Modern philosophy still draws heavily on the works of the ancient Greeks especially Aristotle, Plato and Socrates.

xvii) **philanthropist** (n) (u)   fi-**lan**-thr*uh*-pist

*A person who gives money to good causes (synonym **benefactor**).*

In the ancient world many philanthropists believed that their actions would gain them a better place in the after-life.

xviii) **philistine** (n) (c), (adj.)   **fil**-*uh*-stahyn

A person who has no interest in, or appreciation of culture and the arts. / Describing an attitude of indifference or hostility towards culture.

Lovers of classical music sometimes look down on young people who like punk or rap music and think they are ignorant philistines.

xix) **bibliophile** (n) (c)   **bib**-lee-*uh*-fahyl   *

A person who loves and collects books.

Sir Thomas Bodley was a 17th century bibliophile and **philanthropist** who founded one of the most famous libraries in the world: the Bodleian at Oxford University.

xx) **philharmonic** (adj.)   fil-hahr-**mon**-ik

In music, describing a range of different sounds in harmony, e.g. in an orchestra.

The London Philharmonic Orchestra enjoys a worldwide reputation.

> **Progression words**
>
> bibliophile
>
> philharmonic

5. phobia (L), hostis (G)   "fear", "enemy"

Core words
- hostile
- claustrophobia
- hostilities

xxi) **hostile** (adj.)   **hos**-tahyl

Describing the attitude of a person or organisation which intends to do harm.

Movies about the Battle of Britain often show Spitfires and Hurricanes engaging <u>hostile</u> aircraft.

xxii) **claustrophobia** (n) (u)   klaw-str*uh*-**foh**-bee-*uh*

The condition of being scared of being confined in a small space.

It is impossible to work in a coal mine if you suffer from <u>claustrophobia</u>.

xxiii) **hostilities** (n) (u)   ho-**stil**-i-teez

A state of war between two or more countries.

<u>Hostilities</u> between Britain and Germany broke out on 3rd September 1939.

xxiv) **arachnophobia** (n) (u)   *uh*-rak-n*uh*-**foh**-bee-*uh*

*An extreme, **irrational** fear of spiders.*

People suffering from <u>arachnophobia</u> will scream or jump in the air at the sight of a spider.

xxv) **acrophobia** (n) (u)   ak-ruh-**foh**-bee-uh

A fear of heights.

He could not get the cat down from the tree because of his <u>acrophobia</u>.

Progression words
- arachnophobia
- acrophobia

6. sens/senti (L) "feel"

Core words
- assent
- resent
- sensitive

xxvi) **assent** (v) (I), (n) (u)   uh-**sent**

To agree to an idea or proposal. / agreement, cf. dissent.

In the United States the President has to give his assent to all new laws before they can take effect.

xxvii) **resent** (v) (T)   ri-**zent**

To feel annoyed that something has happened.

A lot of students resent the university's decision to increase accommodation fees in the halls of residence.

xxviii) **sensitive** (adj.)   **sen**-si-tiv

*Describing something which is easily affected by emotional feelings or physical pain, cf. **insensitive**.*

Some students are sensitive to criticism of their work and find it hard to accept it.

xxix) **consensus** (n) (u)   kuh n-**sen**-suh s

*An agreement between a **multitude** of people, often the result of negotiation and compromise.*

After extensive negotiations the group reached a consensus to locate the company's new headquarters in Bonn.

xxx) **sentimentally** (adv.)   sen-tuh-**men**-tlee

A manner of doing something which shows feelings.

The old man spoke sentimentally about his boyhood in a remote Indian village.

Progression words
- consensus
- sentimentally

N.B.

Adverbs

In the first five units of this book we have concentrated on nouns, verbs and adjectives but roots can also be used as adverbs. These indicate something about how the action of a verb was performed. For example:

ii) **amicably**
v) **amorously**
xiii) **sympathetically**
xxx) **sentimentally**

Nearly all such adverbs have an equivalent adjective but not all adjectives have an equivalent adverb. Review the word families we have created in earlier units and add adverbs where appropriate.

Suffixes

In Units 1-5 we have met a number of suffixes which can be combined with roots. Review Unit 4, Lesson A. In this unit we have met roots which are themselves used as a suffix, e.g.

xxii) claustro<u>phobia</u>   xxiv) arachno<u>phobia</u>

The opposite root **phile**, meaning a lover of something, is also widely used as a suffix, e.g.

xix) **biblio<u>phile</u>**

New words are continually being created using roots in this way. Understanding the meaning of these roots can help you understand such words when you encounter them in news reports or academic articles.

Section B: Unit 6, Exercises

Exercise 1: Synonyms and antonyms

Choose the best synonym or antonym to replace the underlined word in each sentence. Some words come from previous units to help you review.

1. (   ) Andrew Carnegie was a <u>benefactor</u> who donated millions of dollars to found art galleries in his native USA. (synonym).

    a) psychologist   b) philistine   c) vocalist   d) philanthropist

2. (   ) The directors expressed their <u>assent</u> to/from the proposal to open 20 new stores this year. (antonym).

    a) agreement   b) propose   c) dissent   d) apathy

3. (   ) Fans at the back of the festival site complained that the music was <u>audible</u>. (antonym).

    a) inaudible   b) iraudible   c) visual   d) disaudible

4. (   ) Museums usually feature items of cultural heritage such as pottery or coins which <u>can be touched</u>. (synonym).

    a) are sympathetic   b) are tangible   c) are egotistical   d) are amorous

5. (   ) My friend Lucy has a lovely <u>face</u> and wants to be a model. (synonym).

    a) odour   b) ego   c) visage   d) vista

6. (   ) Many footballers learn to be <u>sensitive</u> to the abuse they get from the crowd and just ignore it. (antonym).

    a) insensitive   d) ultra sensitive   c) illsensitive   d) antisensitive

7. (   ) Tourist attractions need a range of <u>facilities</u> such as hotels, restaurants, information centres and tour guides. (synonym).

    a) audiences   b) philanthropists   c) amenities   d) libraries

Exercise 2: Crossword

Use words from this unit to solve the clues in the box below.

Across
5. Describing something which is not broken
6. A chemical which removes smells
8. A person who is obsessed with themselves
9. The study of the sounds and pronunciation of languages
10. A type of orchestra

Down
1. To feel annoyed about a decision that has been taken
2. Describing a performance which is very poor
3. A lawyer who speaks for others in court
4. A voice and appearance test for actors
7. To charm or captivate somebody

Exercise 3: Sentence completion (collocations)

Complete the sentences below with an appropriate word from this unit. The root is given to help you.

1. Social workers listened ……………………….. (path) to the stories of homeless people.

2. Nitrogen is an ……………………. (odour) gas which makes up approximately 80% of the Earth's atmosphere.

3. Cinema …………………… (aud) loved the slapstick comedy of Laurel and Hardy.

4. On 7th December 1941 the Japanese bombed Pearl Harbour causing ………………….. (host) to break out between the United States and Japan.

5. YouTube is now the most popular and the most controversial …………………….. (vid) sharing platform in the world.

6. Biologists study the ……………………. (centric) behaviour of animals and birds when there is a scarcity of food.

7. Research shows that parents reading aloud with young children helps them develop a wider ……………………. (voc).

8. Climbing the Eiffel Tower in Paris is expensive but worth it for the spectacular ……………… (vis) available from the upper viewing platform.

Vocabulary from Classical Roots

Section B: Unit 7, Lesson A – Colours
1. color (L), chro/chrom/chros (G)   "colour"

Core words

monochrome

multicoloured

discoloured

i) **monochrome** (adj.)   **mon**-*uh*-krohm

    Describing something which uses only a single colour.

    Desert landscapes tend to be a <u>monochrome</u> yellow colour.

ii) **multicoloured** (adj.)   muhl-tee-**kuhl**-er-d

    Describing something which uses several colours.

    At Paris fashion week the latest style is <u>multicoloured</u> dresses and skirts.

iii) **discolour** (v) (T)   dis-**kuhl**-er

    To remove or damage the colour of something.

    I am so angry because my new washing machine faded and <u>discoloured</u> all my expensive clothes.

iv) **chromium** (n) (u)   **kroh**-mee-*uh* m

    A hard, shiny metal element.

    1950s American **automobiles** were often covered with <u>chromium.</u>

v) **Colorado** (n) (u)   kol-*uh*-**rad**-doh

    A state in the west of the USA.

    <u>Colorado</u> gets its name from is distinctive red and yellow rock formations.

Progression words

chromium

Colorado

2. alb (L), aspr (G), leuk (G)   "white"

Core words
- albino
- diaper
- aspirin

vi) **albino** (adj.)   al-**bee**-noh

Describing something which is unusually white.

<u>Albino</u> animals are occasionally found in the wild but they are easy targets for predators because they lack camouflage.

vii) **diaper** (n) (c)   **dahy**-per

A baby's nappy.

<u>Diapers</u> were traditionally made from bleached white cloth.

viii) **aspirin** (n) (u)   **as**-prin

A medicine used as a painkiller.

<u>Aspirin</u> is one of the most widely used pain killers and the tablets are usually white.

ix) **leukaemia** (n) (u)   loo-**kee**-mee-*uh*

A serious disease caused by overproduction of damaged white blood cells.

The number of cases of <u>leukaemia,</u> particularly in children, is increasing in some places but nobody is sure why.

x) **leucine** (n) (u)   **loo**-seen

A type of water-soluble amino acid essential for human nutrition.

<u>Leucine</u> was first isolated in the early 19th century which represented a considerable advance in knowledge of the human digestive system.

Progression words
- leukaemia
- leucine

Vocabulary from Classical Roots

3. melan (G), nigr (L)   "black", "dark"   *

> **Core words**
> melancholy
> melodrama
> denigrate

xi) **melancholy** (n) (u)   **mel**-*uh*n-kol-ee

The condition of feeling sad or depressed.

It is usual to feel melancholy after the death of a loved one.

xii) **melodrama** (n) (c)   **mel**-*uh*-drah-m*uh*

A type of theatrical play or other performance which exaggerates emotions, usually sad emotions.

Nowadays it is fashionable to appear cool and calm and avoid melodrama in public performances such as business presentations and news conferences.

xiii) **denigrate** (v) (T)   **den**-i-greyt

To talk about somebody in a disrespectful, negative way.

Managers should never denigrate a **subordinate** in front of his/her peers.

xiv) **melanoma** (n) (c)   mel-*uh*-**noh**-m*uh*   *

*A tumour on the skin which may be **benign** or malignant.*

Anybody who thinks they may have a melanoma should see a doctor urgently.

xv) **melanin** (n) (u)   **mel**-*uh*-nin

A dark brown to black pigment found in human hair and skin.

Loss of melanin leads to older people's hair turning grey but it can be replaced with artificial dyes.

> **Progression words**
> melanoma
> melanin

Vocabulary from Classical Roots

4. cirr (G), pyrrh (G) rhod (G), rub (L)   "orange", "red"

Core words
Pyrrhic
ruby
rhododendron

xvi) **Pyrrhic** (adj.)   **pir**-ik

*Describing a victory that is not worth winning because it ends in fire
In fire and destruction for both parties.*

Many people believe that World War I was a Pyrrhic victory for Britain because the cost in lives and destruction outweighed the gains.

xvii) **ruby** (n) (c)   **roo**-bee

A dark red gemstone. / A shade of red.

It is traditional to give a gift of something made with rubies on a couple's 40th wedding anniversary.

xviii) **rhododendron** (n) (c)   roh-d*uh*-**den**-dr*uh* n

A species of plant with red or pink flowers.

Rhododendrons were first imported to Europe from China in the 18th century.

xix) **cirrhosis** (n) (u)   si-**roh**-sis   *

A serious disease of the liver which makes it appear orange.

Cirrhosis of the liver is a common consequence of alcoholism and is usually fatal.

xx) **rubella** (n) (u)   roo-**bel**-*uh*   *

*A **contagious** disease, popularly known as German measles, characterised by red spots.*

Governments try to ensure that all children are vaccinated against rubella.

Progression words
cirrhosis
rubella

123

5. chlor (G), cyan/ sapphir (G)   "green", "blue"

Core words
- chlorine
- cyan
- sapphire

xxi) **chlorine** (n) (u)   **klawr**-een

A heavy, greenish yellow gas.

Chlorine is often added to the water in swimming pools to keep it clean.

xxii) **cyan** (n) (u)   **sahy**-an

A shade of blue.

Cyan blue was one of the most fashionable colours for women's clothes and accessories.

xxiii) **sapphire** (n) (c)   **saf**-ahy*uh* r

A blue gemstone. / A shade of blue.

He gave his fiancée a diamond and sapphire engagement ring.

xxiv) **chloroform** (n) (u)   **klawr**-*uh*-fawrm

A greenish coloured liquid once used in medicine as an anaesthetic.

The anaesthetic properties of chloroform were first discovered by the Scottish doctor, Sir James Young Simpson in the 1870s.

xxv) **cyanide** (n) (u)   **sahy**-*uh*-nahyd

A highly poisonous chemical which in its pure form is blue.

Cyanide is one of the most toxic substances known to humanity but is also useful for extracting pure gold from ore.

Progression words
- chloroform
- cyanide

6. argent (L), aur / chrysto (G)   "silver", "gold"

Core words
- aura
- aureole
- chrysanthemum

xxvi) aura (n) (c)   **awr**-*uh*

A pervasive and radiant quality of character.

In ancient times radiance of an <u>aura</u> was associated with shiny metals especially gold.

xxvii) aureole (n) (c)   **awr**-ee-ohl

A circle of light, also known as a halo painted around the head of a holy person.

In Medieval Christian art the <u>aureole</u> of a saint was nearly always painted in gold.

xxviii) chrysanthemum (n) (c)   kri-**san**-th*uh*-m*uh* m

A popular plant of the daisy family whose flowers are **multicoloured** *but have a yellow centre.*

<u>Chrysanthemums</u> are popular with gardeners like my grandfather because they make a colourful display.

xxix) Argentina (n) (c)   ahr-j*uh* n-**tee**-n*uh*

A country in South America.

When Spanish explorers discovered <u>Argentina</u> in the early 16th century, they expected to find huge deposits of silver but were disappointed.

Progression words
- Argentina
- chrysalis

xxx) chrysalis (n) (c)   **kris**-*uh*-lis

A hard shell surrounding the pupa of a moth.

The silk clothes made from thread unwound from silkworm <u>chrysalises</u> were extremely expensive in ancient Rome and worth their weight in gold.

N.B.

Register

English did not need to borrow Latin and Greek roots to make words for everyday things such as colours because it did not need to. It already had a stock of indigenous words from Germanic languages and Norman French. However, the Renaissance intellectuals who laid the foundations of modern science and medicine needed to persuade people that their new knowledge was out of the ordinary, scarce and thus financially valuable. Hence, they created new words from Greek and Latin roots to give their learning credibility, so we find formal colour words in science and medicine.

Chains of Reasoning

In most societies, colours have cultural connotations. These are not constant across cultures and can change over time.

3. **melan "black":** In the ancient world the colour black had strong negative connotations concerned with pain, sadness, death and the afterlife hence words such as

   xi) **melancholy** "a feeling of sadness"

Accuracy

While understanding the roots of words can give you a clue as to their meaning, the roots do not always accord precisely with modern science. For example, ancient and Renaissance doctors did not have all the scientific tests available today and one of the few ways they could diagnose illness was by the colour of body parts hence:

xiv) **melanoma**   xix) **cirrhosis**   xx) **rubella**

Modern doctors have more precise methods but the old vocabulary is still used for the sake of consistency.

Section B: Unit 7, Lesson B – Motion and Transport

1. aer/aero (G)   "air", "atmosphere"

i) **aerospace** (n) (u), (adj.)   **air**-oh-speys

The earth's atmosphere and space beyond it considered together. / The industry which develops aircraft and spacecraft.

The aerospace industry is a major employer of skilled workers in developed countries.

Core words
- aerospace
- aerosol
- aerated

ii) **aerosol** (n) (c)   **air**-uh-sawl

A means of delivering chemicals from a metal container under pressure.

Aerosol sprays are a common method of applying **deodorants.**

iii) **aerated** (adj.)   **air**-yet-id

Describing something which has air circulated through it.

One of the first aerated drinks was invented by John Stith Pemberton who called it Coca Cola.

iv) **aerodynamics** (n) (u)   air-oh-dahy-**nam**-iks

The science of making objects pass through air more efficiently.

Formula 1 cars depend heavily on aerodynamics to achieve high performance.

v) **aeroelastic materials** (n) (plural)   air-oh- ih-**las**-tik m*uh*-**teer**-ee-*uh*l s

A group of materials which change their shape in response to the pressure of air flowing over them.

Theoretically, aeroelastic materials can reduce drag and therefore allow cars or aircraft to achieve higher performance using less fuel.

Progression words
- aerodynamics
- aeroelastic materials

2. cycl (G), cylind (G), helic (G)   "roll", "circle", "spiral"

Core words
- cyclical
- helicopter
- tricycle

vi) **cyclical** (adj.)   **sahy**-kli-k*uh* l

Describing something which fluctuates according to a regular pattern over time.

Economies grow and contract in a cyclical pattern known as the business cycle.

vii) **helicopter** (n) (c)   **hel**-i-kop-ter

A type of aircraft which uses rotating wings to gain lift.

Helicopters play a vital role in search and rescue missions because they can hover and fly in confined spaces.

viii) **tricycle** (n) (c)   **trahy**-si-k*uh* l

A vehicle with three wheels driven by either pedal power or an engine.

Motorized tricycles are widely used for making deliveries in the narrow streets of developing countries.

ix) **cyclone** (n) (c)   **sahy**-klohn

An air mass in the atmosphere with low pressure and circular wind motion.

Cyclones are common in the earth's weather systems but can be very powerful and destructive.

x) **helix** (n) (c)   **hee**-liks

Something wrapped around a cylinder.

The coil springs on cars are formed by wrapping a steel tube around a cylinder to make a helix.

Progression words
- cyclone
- helix

128

3. mob (L)   "move"

Core words
- mobile
- mobility
- automobile

xi) **mobile** (adj.)   moh-b*uhy* l

Describing something which can easily move or be moved.

<u>Mobile</u> mechanics are self-employed experts who travel to where a vehicle has broken down instead of it being towed to their premises.

xii) **mobility** (n) (u)   moh-**bil**-i-tee

The condition of being able to move.

In sociology, the term <u>social mobility</u> refers to the ability of individuals to move from one social class to another.

xiii) **automobile** (n) (c)   aw-t*uh*-m*uh*-**beel**

A car.

The invention of the <u>automobile</u> in 1885 led to a revolution in personal **mobility**.

xiv) **immobilize** (v) (T)   ih-**moh**-b*uh*-lahyz

To make something impossible to move.

Doctors will sometimes <u>immobilize</u> a patient with a neck or back injury to prevent paralysis.

xv) **mob** (n) (u), (v) (T)   mob

A large crowd of people, usually violent. / The action of many people surrounding someone usually to intimidate.

The rulers of ancient Rome always feared the <u>mob</u> which had the ability to move quickly from place to place causing trouble.

Progression words
- immobilize
- mob

4. mot/mov/mut (L)   "move", "motion"

Core words
- motion
- motorize
- commute

xvi) motion (n) (c), (v) (T)   **moh**-sh*uh* n

Movement from place to place. / The action of making a hand gesture or signal.

Renaissance scientists were fascinated by the idea of continuous <u>motion</u> machines but never succeeded in building one.

xvii) motorize (v) (T)   **moh**-t*uh*-rahyz

To add a motor to an existing object.

In the First World War all the combatants tried to <u>motorize</u> their military transport.

xviii) commute (v) (I)   k*uh*-**myoot**

The action of travelling to work, school or college every day.

The design of modern cities means that most workers have to <u>commute</u> every day.

xix) locomotive (n) (c)   loh-k*uh*-**moh**-tiv

A formal word for a railway engine.

A Cornish engineer, Richard Trevithick, invented the <u>locomotive</u> in 1805.

xx) immutable (adj.)   ih-**myoo**-t*uh*-b*uh* l

Describing something which can never be moved or changed.

The ancient Greeks and Romans believed that the laws of nature are <u>immutable</u> principles.

Progression words
- locomotive
- immutable

5. naut (G), nav (L)   "ship"

> **Core words**
> naval
> navigate
> nausea

xxi) naval (adj.)   ney-v*uh* l

Describing something related to ships used in war.

The ancient Athenians were the greatest naval power in the **Mediterranean.**

xxii) navigate (v) (T)   **nav**-i-geyt

The action of finding the correct route to a destination across the sea or sky.

Ancient sailors could navigate by using the positions of the sun and the stars.

xxiii) nausea (n) (u)   **naw**-zee-*uh*

The condition of feeling sick.

Julius Caesar and his **centurions** probably suffered from nausea, also called sea sickness, when crossing the English Channel to invade Britain in 55BC.

xxiv) nautical (adj.)   **naw**-ti-k*uh*l

Describing something to do with the sea or sailors.

Distances at sea are measured in unique units including the nautical mile (1.852 kilometres).

xxv) astronaut (n) (c)   **as**-tr*uh*-nawt

A person who travels in a spaceship.

Astronauts, who spend long periods working on the International Space Station, experience a range of health effects.

> **Progression words**
> nautical
> astronaut

6. port (L)   "carry"

Core words
- port
- import
- export

xxvi) **port** (n) (c)   pawrt

A place where ships dock to load or unload.

Rotterdam in the Netherlands is now the world's busiest port.

xxvii) **import** (n) (u)(c)   **im**-pawrt

Goods and services brought into a country from abroad, cf. exports.

In Britain, the value of imports usually exceeds the value of **exports** hence the country has a balance of payments deficit.

xxviii) **export** (v) (T)   ik-**spawrt**

The action of sending goods from one country to another. / The action of sending data to another program.

The researcher could not export the file containing his data to his fellow scientists' computers because it was corrupted.

xxix) **portable** (adj.)   **pawr**-t*uh*-b*uh* l

*Describing something which is **mobile** and can be easily carried by hand.*

Laptop computers are portable but mainframes are **immobile**.

xxx) **reporter** (n) (c)   ri-**pawr**-ter

A person who collects and transmits news for a media (radio, TV, etc.) .

Newspapers existed in ancient Rome but we do not know much about their reporters.

Progression words
- portable
- reporter

N.B.

Reminder: Collocations and compounds

One of the best ways to learn to use new words in sentences is to make notes of collocations (words often used together) and compound nouns (noun + noun).

In this lesson you will find several examples of adjective + noun collocations and compounds used with root words.

Adjective + noun

ii) aerospace industry vi) cyclical pattern
viii) motorized tricycles xii) social mobility

Compounds

iii) aerosol spray
xi) mobile mechanic

Review the lesson and add any others you can find.

More than one root

Remember English words can include more than one Greek or Latin root. This is particularly common where one of the roots is a core concept such as numbers and negatives, e.g.

viii) tricycle xiv) immobilize

Review Lesson A and add other examples.

Second roots used in other words in this unit will be explained in later units:

iii) aerosol (unit 10) xiii) automobile (unit 9)

Vocabulary from Classical Roots

Section B: Unit 7, Exercises
Exercise 1: Labelling diagrams and pictures

Match each picture with a word from the boxes.

a) ....

b) ....

c) ....

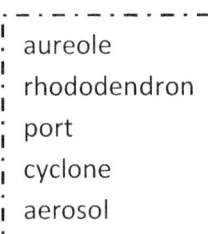

```
aureole
rhododendron
port
cyclone
aerosol
```

d) ....

e) ....

f) ....

g) ....

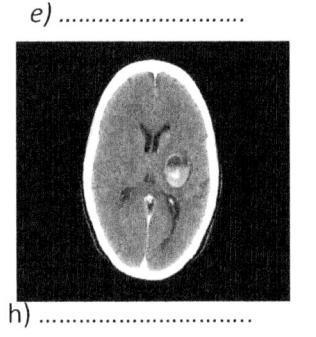

h) ....

```
reporter
melanoma
locomotive
Argentina
helicopter
```

i) ....

j) ....

Vocabulary from Classical Roots

Exercise 2: Multiple choice, collocations, context and synonyms

Choose the best answer for each of the following questions:

1. (   ) In which of the following contexts would you expect to encounter the word *rubella*?

    a) math   b) chemistry   c) transport   d) medicine

2. (   ) A ………………….. mile is a measurement of distance used at sea.

    a) naval   b) nautical   c) automobile   d) navigation

3. (   ) The Greeks and Romans believed that laws of nature such as gravity
    are …………………… principles of physics.

    a) immutable   b) irrational   c) immobilizable   d) importable

4. (   ) In which two of the following contexts might you find aerodynamics useful?

    (   ) a) medicine   b) aerospace engineering   c) Formula 1   d) art

5. (   ) WWI armies replaced horses with ……………………….. transport for the first time.

    a) locomotive   b) naval   c) helicoptor   d) motorized

6. (   ) In which industry might a company manufacture something aerated:

    a) food and drink   b) automotive   c) import and export d) aerospace

7. (   ) Sea sickness is an every day term for a condition also called …………………….

    a) rubella   b) nausea   c) chrysalis   d) cyanide

8. (   ) The inventions of the first bicycle and then the automobile gave rise to a revolution in
    personal ……………………..

    a) commute   b) portability   c) mobility   d) health

Vocabulary from Classical Roots

Exercise 3: Fill in the Blanks

Choose the best word from the box to fill in the blanks in the following passage.

automobile
navigate
exports
locomotive
commuting
tricycles
astronauts
ports

Changes in transport have been one of biggest drivers of globalization in the last five centuries. In the ancient and medieval worlds sailors could not venture very far from the coast because they could only (1) .... by using the sun and the stars. The developments of new instruments and mathematical techniques in the 15th century changed that and intrepid explorers such as Christopher Columbus and Ferdinad Magellan set out to explore the world. They returned to European (2) .... ,often years later, and unloaded an astonishing array of new products including things we now take for granted such as coffee and tomatoes never before seen in Europe. This produced a rapid expansion in international trade and both imports and (3) .... accelerated further with the development of factories and steam ships in the 19th century.

Steam also provided the motive power for the next major breakthrough, the invention of the (4) .... which could pull heavy loads along a set of parallel iron rails. That drove the industrial revolution and as cities got bigger and workers had to live further from their workplaces the need for personal mobility increased. Bicycles were one answer and three wheeled variants called (5) .... were also used to deliver everything from ice cream to parcels, as they still are in developing countries.

Steam and pedal power were superceded in the 20th century by the internal combustion engine which allowed the development of the (6) .... Once cars were mass produced and affordable after the 1920s, personal mobility became available to almost everyone in developed countries. But it has come at a price. As cities have become designed around cars most workers now have to spend hours (7) .... and parking, pollution and other drawbacks are becoming ever more apparent. Not surprisingly, some people fantasize about the next transport revolution, space travel and (8) .... have become as much folk heroes as the explorers and railway engineers were in their day.

Section B: Unit 8, Lesson A – Common Verbs 1

1. form (L)   "shape"

Core words
conform
deform
reform

i) **conform** (v) (T)   k*uh*n-**fawrm**

To act in accordance with norms, standards or regulations.

Norms of acceptable behaviour to which most people <u>conform</u> give society shape and cohesion.

ii) **deform** (v) (T)   dih-**fawrm**

To cause something to lose or change its shape.

The amount of force which a material can withstand before it <u>deforms</u> can be measured by stress tests and is crucial in engineering and construction.

iii) **reform** (v) (T)   ri-**fawrm**

To change something in a way which improves it.

Many countries face demands to <u>reform</u> their laws on women's rights.

iv) **formula** (n) (c)   **fawr**-my*uh*-luh

A mathematical expression in algebra or geometry. / An expression of the chemical composition of a substance.

The system of standard written chemical <u>formulas</u> was developed in the 19th century by the Swedish chemist Jöns Jakob Berzelius.

v) **formulate** (v) (T)   **fawr**-my*uh*-leyt

To shape ideas into a theory. / To precisely define the ingredients required to make a substance.

Pharmaceutical companies have to <u>formulate</u> new drugs very carefully to ensure patient safety.

Progression words
formula
formulate

2. pati/pass (L)   "suffer", "feel"

Core words

passion

compassion

patient

vi) **passion** (n) (c)   **pash**-*uh*n

Strong feelings or emotions.

In Shakespeare's play Romeo and Juliet are willing to risk everything because of their passion for each other.

vii) **compassion** (n) (u)   k*uh*m-**pash**-*uh*n

A feeling of sympathy for those who have experienced misfortune.

Some people feel compassion for refugees displaced by war or political persecution.

viii) **patient** (adj.)   **pey**-sh*uh*nt

Describing somebody who accepts delay or inconvenience without complaint, or gives others time to complete a task.

The class loved Ms Jones because she was always patient with students who were struggling to keep up with the course.

ix) **dispassionate** (adj.)   dis-**pash**-*uh*-nit

Describing something done, or said without personal feeling or emotion.

The newsreader's voice was completely dispassionate despite the scale of the destruction caused by Hurricane Betty.

x) **impassioned** (adj.)   im-**pash**-*uh*nd

Describing something filled with intense feeling.

Greta Thunberg has made a series of impassioned pleas for more urgent action to halt climate change.

Progression words

dispassionate

impassioned

3. migr (L)   "move"

Core words
- migrate
- emigrate
- immigration

xi) migrate (v) (I)   **mahy**-greyt

To move from one place to another temporarily or permanently.

Animals, birds and people all <u>migrate</u> for a variety of reasons.

xii) emigrate (v) (I)   **em**-i-greyt

To leave one's country of birth and settle in another country.

Tens of millions of people have <u>emigrated</u> from Europe to the Americas over the last five hundred years.

xiii) immigration (n) (u)   im-i-**grey**-sh*uh*n

The process or phenomenon of people arriving in a country from elsewhere aiming to settle.

<u>Immigration</u> from developing to developed countries is one of the most contentious issues in modern politics.

xiv) migratory (adj.)   **mahy**-gr*uh*-tawr-ee

In biology, describing a species which regularly moves from one habitat to another.

Swallows are migratory birds which spend their winters in Africa and their summers in the UK.

xv) émigré (n) (c)   **em**-i-grey

A person who has fled from their native country, usually as a result of war or persecution.

The Huguenots were Protestant <u>émigrés</u> from France who settled in the UK in the late 17th century.

Progression words
- migratory
- émigré

4. spec/spect (L)   "see", "look"

Core words
- spectator
- introspective
- prospective

xvi) **spectator** (n) (c), (adj.)   spek-**tey**-ter

A person who watches others do something.

Football is by far the most popular spectator sport in the world.

xvii) **introspective** (adj.)   in-tr*uh*-**spek**-tiv

Describing a person who looks into themselves.

Psychology teaches that being introspective can be positive if it is part of a process of learning from one's mistakes, or negative if it involves shunning social contact.

xviii) **prospective** (adj.)   pr*uh*-**spek**-tiv

Describing somebody who may do something in the future./ Something likely to happen in future.

Universities often reach out to prospective students by inviting them to open days.

xix) **conspicuous** (adj.)   k*uh*n-**spik**-yoo-*uh*s

Describing something which is easy to see.

In some cultures, the rich engage in conspicuous consumption in order to show off wealth and taste.

xx) **circumspect** (adj.)   sur-k*uh*m-spekt

Describing a person who is being cautious.

Some businesses need to be very circumspect about announcing the earnings of their CEO.

Progression words
- conspicuous
- circumspect

5. tract (L) "pull", "drag"

Core words
- detract
- distract
- tractor

xxi) detract (v) (T) dih-**trakt**

To decrease the value or reputation of something.

The professor said that logical fallacies <u>detracted</u> from the validity of the student's arguments.

xxii) distract (v) (T) dih-**strakt**

To do something which drags another person's attention away from what they were doing.

Teachers complain that mobile phones <u>distract</u> student's attention from their studies.

xxiii) tractor (n) (c) **trak**-ter

*A **motorized** vehicle used for pulling farm machinery.*

Porsche are famous for **manufacturing** sports cars but they also made <u>tractors</u> in the 1950s.

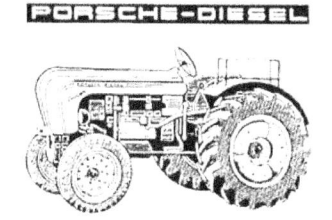

xxiv) traction (n) (u) **trak**-sh*uh* n

The mechanical quality of being able to grip and pull strongly. / Something which is gaining credibility and popularity.

Engineers seek to maximise the <u>traction</u> of a racing car so that it can accelerate hard out of a corner.

xxv) tract (n) (c) trakt

An old-fashioned word for a short book written to pull or persuade readers towards the writer's point of view.

Religious <u>tracts</u> made up the majority of all books printed in 16th and 17th century Europe.

Progression words
- traction
- tract

141

6. vol (L) "want", "wish"

xxvi) **voluntary** (adj.)   **vol**-*uh*n-ter-ee

> **Core words**
> voluntary
> volunteer
> volition

Describing something which a person wants to do or chooses to do of their own free will.

Some people choose to do voluntary work to give something back to society.

xxvii) **volunteer** (v), (n) (c)   vol-*uh* n-**teer**

To agree to do a task that is not required or which is unpaid. / A person who chooses to do tasks they do not have to do or are not paid for.

Military officers will sometimes ask individuals to volunteer for particularly dangerous tasks rather than ordering a whole unit to carry them out.

xxviii) **volition** (v) (T)   voh-**lish**-*uh*n

The act of willing something to happen or choosing to do something.

The court decided that the Anderson carried out the attack of his own volition and not under duress from a gang leader.

xxix) **malevolent** (adj.)   m*uh*-**lev**-*uh*-l*uh* nt

Describing thoughts or actions intended to harm others.

Tony gave his ex-girlfriend a malevolent stare when they met at the bus stop.

xxx) **involuntary** (adj.)   in-**vol**-*uh*n-ter-ee

Describing an action which a person is unable to control.

Patients suffering from epilepsy suffer involuntary convulsions of their bodies.

> **Progression words**
> malevolent
> involuntary

N.B.

Study skills: Root trees

As we have seen in earlier units, many Greek and Latin roots are used to form families of words in English when combined with various prefixes and suffixes. Root trees are a useful way of helping you extend and learn these families.

Example

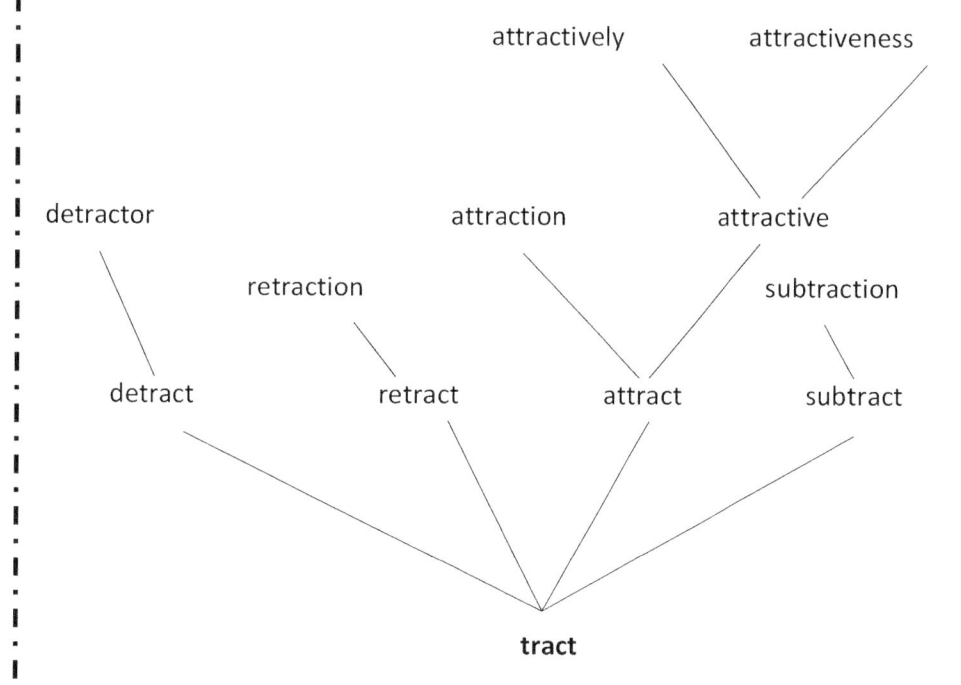

```
              attractively    attractiveness
                    \              /
                     \            /
    detractor       attraction   attractive
         \              |            \
          \         retraction      subtraction
           \            |              |
          detract    retract   attract   subtract
              \         \        |        /
               \         \       |       /
                \         \      |      /
                          tract
```

Review units 1-7 and try to make similar trees for other roots.

Tip:

It is sometimes easier to do this kind of brainstorming activity with a study partner.

Section B: Unit 8, Lesson B – Common Verbs 2
1. capt/cept/ceive (L)   "take", "hold"

Core words
capture
perceive
recipient

i) **capture** (v) (T)   kap-cher

To take control of something or someone.

Aerospace companies such as Boeing and Airbus struggle to <u>capture</u> the largest possible market share for their products.

ii) **perceive** (v) (T)   per-**seev**

To recognise and understand something.

Nowadays businesses collect and analyse huge amounts of electronic data in order to <u>perceive</u> new trends among their customers as quickly as possible.

iii) **recipient** (n) (c)   ri-**sip**-ee-*uh* nt

A person who receives and takes ownership of something.

NGOs often try to monitor the <u>recipients</u> of international aid after disasters.

iv) **captivate** (v) (T)   **kap**-t*uh*-veyt

To take control of a person's affections. / To attract somebody's attention.

In Charlotte Bronte's novel, Jane Eyre, the heroine is <u>captivated</u> by her employer, Mr Rochester.

v) **intercept** (v) (T)   in-ter-**sept**

To gain access to something which is being passed or communicated between two other parties.

In war, countries try to <u>intercept</u> messages being sent by the enemies' armed forces.

Progression words
captivate
intercept

Vocabulary from Classical Roots

2. miss (L)   "send", "let go"

Core words
- mission
- admission
- dismiss

vi) **mission** (n) (c)   mish-*uh* n

An operation in business, war or religion carried out by a group of people sent to another place.

USAF bomber crews in World War II usually carried out 30-40 missions before being rested.

vii) **admission** (n) (c), (u)   ad-**mish**-*uh* n

The right to gain entry to something. / A statement in which a person accepts that they did something wrong.

Some museums give free admission to children in an attempt to provide educational opportunities. / The burglar was given a reduced sentence in return for his full admission of guilt.

viii) **dismiss** (v) (T)   dis-**mis**

To reject an idea or suggestion. / To fire somebody from their job.

The Prime minister dismissed suggestions that he was about to raise taxes. / The chief cashier was dismissed for fraud.

ix) **missile** (n) (c)   **mis**-ahyl

An unmanned weapon capable of being fired remotely to hit a target some distance away.

Wernher von Braun designed the world's first missile, the German V2 rocket in 1944.

x) **missive** (n) (c)   **mis**-iv

An official letter, usually pleading for some action to be taken.

Campaigners against the new bypass angrily **dismissed** the latest missive from the council asking them to withdraw their objections.

Progression words
- missile
- missive

3. quer/quir/quesit (L)   "search", "seek"

Core words
- acquire
- inquiry
- conquer

xi) **acquire** (v) (T)   *uh-**kwahy**uh r*

To gain or obtain something.

When people move house they are usually surprised at how much stuff they have <u>acquired</u> over the years.

xii) **inquiry** (n) (c)   *in-**kwahy**uhr-ee*

A formal procedure to seek out the facts about an issue.

The public <u>inquiry</u> into proposals to build a new runway at the city's airport has cost millions of dollars.

xiii) **conquer** (v) (T)   ***kong**-ker*

*To **capture** another country by force. / To overcome adversity.*

Alexander the Great sought to <u>conquer</u> the entire world, as it was known to the ancient Greeks, and nearly succeeded.

xiv) **prerequisite** (n) (c)   *pri-**rek**-wuh-zit*

Something which is required before something else can happen.

In the USA, a very high SAT score is a <u>prerequisite</u> for **admission** to an Ivy League university.

xv) **requisition** (v) (T), (n) (c)   *rek-wuh-**zish**-uh n*

To acquire something by order of the state. / An order to hand over something.

In World War I armies <u>requisitioned</u> millions of horses for transport before they were able to **motorize**.

Progression words
- prerequisite
- requisition

Vocabulary from Classical Roots

4. serv (L)   "save", "keep", "serve"

> **Core words**
> preserve
> conserve
> reservation

xvi) **preserve** (v) (T)   pri-**zurv**

To keep something safe and in existence.

UNESCO World Heritage sites were created to <u>preserve</u> and make accessible the most important aspects of the world's cultural heritage.

xvii) **conserve** (v) (T)   con-**zurv**

To save something, usually for use at a later date.

Businesses are under pressure to <u>conserve</u> energy to protect the environment and reduce costs.

xviii) **reservation** (n) (c)   rez-er-**vey**-sh*uh* n

Something kept back for a particular person and no longer available to others.

The secretary told her boss she had made a <u>reservation</u> for him at the best hotel during the World Economic Forum in Davos.

xix) **servile** (adj.)   **sur**-vahyl

Describing a person who is eager to please or is in slavery.

The ancient Romans sometimes kept captured soldiers in <u>servile</u> conditions for many years.

xx) **subservient** (adj.)   s*uh* b-**sur**-vee-*uh* nt

Describing a person who is answerable to a superior.

For thousands of years common people were <u>subservient</u> to royalty in most societies.

> **Progression words**
> servile
> subservient

5. stru/struct (L)   "build"

Core words
construct
structure
destruction

xxi) **construct** (v) (T), (n) (c)   k**uh**n-**struhkt** (v) **kon**-struhkt (n)

The action of building something. / A complex theory or academic term built up by combining simpler ideas.

In sociology, "community" is a contested <u>construct</u>.

xxii) **structure** (n) (c), (v) (T)   **struhk**-cher

A way of organising materials or ideas. / The action of organising materials or ideas.

Understanding the molecular <u>structure</u> of materials, such as steel or plastic, is an important part of material science.

xxiii) **destruction** (n) (u)   dih-**struhk**-sh*uh* n

The process of destroying, or trashing something.

Forces of nature, such as **cyclones,** can cause massive <u>destruction</u>.

xxiv) **construe** (v) (T)   **kon**-stroo

To infer a meaning or conclusion from a written passage.

My grandfather told me that when he was a boy, high school students had to <u>construe</u> a passage of Latin every day for homework.

xxv) **infrastructure** (n) (u)   **in**-fr*uh*-struhk-cher

Constructed facilities which hold a country and its economy together.

Investments in <u>infrastructure</u> such as roads, railways, electricity grids and sewage systems are essential for the development of poor countries.

Progression words
construe
infrastructure

6. tort (L)   "twist"

Core words
- contortions
- distort
- extort

xxvi) **contortions** (n) (plural)   k*uh* n-**tawr**-sh*uh* n

Something twisted into complex shapes.

Some ballet dancers can perform amazing <u>contortions</u>.

xxvii) **distort** (v) (T)   dih-**stawrt**

To twist or force something into an unnatural shape. / To interfere with evidence to give a misleading impression of the truth.

News **reporters** are often accused of <u>distorting</u> the facts to fit their personal prejudices.

xxviii) **extort** (v) (T)   ik-**stawrt**

To obtain money or benefits by threatening somebody.

The mafia <u>extort</u> money from businesses by threatening violence against their employees or attacks on their premises.

xxix) **torsion** (n) (u)   **tawr**-sh*uh* n

In engineering the twisting force required to loosen or tighten something.

It is important for safety to apply the correct amount of <u>torsion</u> to the wheel nuts of a car.

xxx) **retort** (v) (I)   ri-**tawrt**

To reply, usually sharply and immediately.

The ability to come up with a witty <u>retort</u> is an important skill for politicians being interviewed on TV or radio.

Progression words
- torsion
- retort

N.B.

Parts of speech

English words formed from Greek and Latin roots are not always the same part of speech as the original root. The addition of a suffix can change a verb into a noun (called a nominalizer), for example. Therefore, remember to make notes of the part of speech every time you learn a new word.

Context

Some of the progression words in this book are topic specific. That means they are used to talk or write about a particular topic. If you are taking standardized tests, correct use of topic specific vocabulary is very important for high scores, so make note of the topic and context alongside new words in your notebook.

Study Tip:

Make index cards or computer files of words classified by topic, e.g. math terms, engineering terms, argumentative/persuasive terms, learn them in groups and add to them continously as you learn more words.

Section B: Unit 8, Exercises

Exercise 1: Completing a context table

The following table is constructed from topics and words from previous units in this book. Fill in the blanks with words from this unit in the Word-bank.

<u>Note:</u> *Blanks 1 and 3 have been filled in for you.*

<u>Category</u>	Argumentative and persuasive writing and speaking	(1) *engineering*	economics	(2) ....
<u>Topic specific words</u>	equivocal	deform	imports	melancholy
	(3) *retort*	(4)	(5)	(6) ....
	(7)	helix	(8)	megalomania
	admission	(9)	exports	(10) ....

```
                    Word-bank

        infrastructure      engineering

        introspective       retort

        construe            structure

        conserve            circumspect

        personality         torsion
```

151

Exercise 2: Matching definitions

Match the words in column A with the definitions in column B.

	A: Target words		B: Definitions
1.	distract	a)	An adjective used to describe thoughts or actions meant to harm other people.
2.	formulate	b)	A requirement before something else can happen.
3.	extort	c)	Something which is clearly visible.
4.	volunteer	d)	In chemistry, to precisely define the ingredients required to make a substance.
5.	prerequisite	e)	Describing a person who speaks without feeling or emotion.
6.	conspicuous	f)	A species of bird or animal which moves to another place when the seasons change.
7.	malevolent	g)	To gain money or benefits by putting pressure on somebody.
8.	reservation	h)	To agree to undertake something which you do not have to do.
9.	dispassionate	i)	A seat on a train, for example, booked for a particular person and not available for anyone else.
10.	migratory	j)	To divert another person's attention away from what they are doing.

1. ……. 2. …… 3. …… 4. …… 5. …… 6. …… 7. …… 8. …… 9. …… 10. ……

Exercise 3: Collocations

Match the words to make collocations.

Note: The first one has been done for you.

1. ......*g*...... 2. .... 3. .... 4. .... 5. ....

6. .... 7. .... 8. .... 9. .... 10. ....

	Column A		Column B
1	extort	a	retort
2	witty	b	work
3	public	c	formula
4	conquer	d	energy
5	conserve	e	attention
6	free	f	sport
7	attract	g	money
8	spectator	h	a country
9	chemical	i	inquiry
10	voluntary	j	admission

Section B: Unit 9, Lesson A – Common Verbs 3

1. auto (G)   "self-directed", "from within"

> **Core words**
> automatic
> automate
> authentic

i) **automatic** (adj.)   aw-t*uh*-**mat**-ik

Describing something that has the capability to operate independently.

<u>Automatic</u> Telling Machines (ATMs) were first developed by Barclays in the late 1960s and have since become the main method of drawing cash from banks.

ii) **automation** (n) (u)   **aw**-t*uh*-mey-sh*uh* n

The process of replacing human labour with machines.

Experts say that millions of jobs are vulnerable to <u>automation</u> over the next twenty years.

iii) **authentic** (adj.)   aw-**then**-tik

Describing something which is genuine and true to its traditions.

Tourists increasingly want to experience <u>authentic</u> local culture and cuisine when they travel.

iv) **autarky** (n) (c)   **aw**-tahr-kee

The policy of running a country based on self-sufficiency and in isolation from its neighbours.

North Korea is the nearest thing to a true <u>autarky</u> in the modern world.

v) **autobiography** (n) (c)   aw-t*uh*-bahy-**og**-r*uh*-fee

A person's life story written by themselves.

It is increasingly common for business leaders as well as politicians and sports stars to write their <u>autobiographies</u>.

> **Progression words**
> autarky
> autobiography

2. cad/cid/ (L)   "fall", "occur"

Core words
- accident
- coincide
- incident

vi) **accident** (n) (c)   ak-si-d*uh*nt

An event which was not intended to happen, usually with negative consequences.

New health and safety laws have significantly reduced the number of industrial <u>accidents</u>.

vii) **coincide** (v) (T)   koh-in-**sahyd**

Of an event, to occur at the same time as another independent event.

The latest movie about D-Day was launched to <u>coincide</u> with the 70th anniversary of the invasion.

viii) **incident** (n) (c)   **in**-si-d*uh*nt

An event which changes the plot or outcome of something.

A penalty awarded to the basketball team was the only important <u>incident</u> in the 1st half.

ix) **cadaver** (adj.)   k*uh*-**dav**-er

A ghastly looking corpse.

People in the Roman Empire believed in the existence of hell, a form of afterlife which was imagined as being below the earth where dead people became horrible <u>cadavers</u>.

x) **deciduous** (adj.)   dih-**sij**-oo-*uh* s

A kind of tree whose leaves fall off every autumn.

The leaves of <u>deciduous</u> trees turn from green to beautiful shades of brown, russet and gold in the autumn.

Progression words
- cadaver
- deciduous

3. duc/duct (L)   "lead"

> **Core words**
> deduce
> induce
> conducive

xi) **deduce** (v) (T)   dih-**dyoos**

To reach a conclusion from known or assumed facts.

Writers do not always make their meaning clear and the ability to <u>deduce,</u> or infer conclusions from what they do say is a key reading skill for academic study.

xii) **induce** (v) (T)   in-**dyoos**

To encourage somebody to do something by persuasion or offering incentives.

Customers are often <u>induced</u> to buy more of a product by special offers of discounts or free gifts.

xiii) **conducive** (adj.)   k*uh* n-**doo**-siv

Describing conditions favourable to a particular outcome.

The economic and social conditions in Weimar Germany were <u>conducive</u> to the rise of Hitler.

xiv) **conductor** (n) (c)   **kon**-duhkt (n)

A person who leads or controls something.

A <u>conductor</u> such as Herbert von Karajan leads a **philharmonic** orchestra and controls the pace and tone of their playing.

xv) **seduce** (v) (T)   si-**doos**

To lead a person to commit an immoral act.

In Homer's Odyssey, the goddess Circe was able to <u>seduce</u> her enemies and transform them into animals.

> **Progression words**
> conductor
> seduce

4. hab/hib/habit (L)   "have", "to live"

Core words
- inhabit
- exhibit
- prohibit

xvi) **inhabit** (v) (T)   in-**hab**-it

To have a home in a particular place.

In most countries the percentage of the population who inhabit cities has increased dramatically in the last 50 years.

xvii) **exhibit** (v) (T)   ig-**zib**-it

To have a display of something in public.

The marketing department wants to exhibit at the annual trade fair in Guangzhou this year.

xviii) **prohibit** (v) (T)   proh-**hib**-it

To have a law which says that something is not allowed.

Smoking is prohibited in all public places in the city.

xix) **habitat** (n) (c)   **hab**-i-tat

The natural environment in which an animal, plant or bird lives.

Many species have become endangered or extinct as a result of the destruction of natural habitats.

xx) **rehabilitate** (v) (T)   ree-h*uh*-**bil**-i-teyt

To return something or someone to a previous state.

Most penal systems have programs to rehabilitate criminals by teaching them the error of their ways and returning them to society as law-abiding citizens.

Progression words
- habitat
- rehabilitate

5. lev (L) "lift", "raise"

Core words
- elevate
- level-headed
- alleviate

xxi) **elevate** (v) (T)   el-*uh*-veyt

To raise something to a higher level or a greater height.

Monarchs traditionally had the power of **patronage** and could elevate a person to the nobility.

xxii) **level-headed** (adj.)   **lev**-*uh* | **hed**-id

Describing a person who is sensible and remains calm under pressure.

Voters often look for someone who is level-headed when electing a president.

xxiii) **alleviate** (v) (T)   *uh*-**lee**-vee-eyt

To reduce the seriousness of something.

Taking **aspirin** can alleviate the pain of a headache or toothache.

xxiv) **leverage** (n) (u)   **lev**-er-ij

In business, politics or social science the means a person has to influence a situation or decision.

Giant supermarket chains such as Walmart are often accused of having too much leverage over suppliers.

xxv) **levitate** (v) (I)   **lev**-i-teyt

To rise or float above the ground usually by supernatural means.

Stories of deities being able to levitate in the form of walking on water are common in some cultures.

Progression words
- leverage
- levitate

6. misc/mixt (L)   "mix"

Core words
- intermix
- miscellaneous
- remix

xxvi) **intermix** (v) (T)   in-ter-**miks**

The action of mixing two, or more things together.

In cosmopolitan cities people of many nationalities and cultures <u>intermix</u>.

xxvii) **miscellaneous** (adj.)   mis-*uh*-**ley**-nee-*uh*s

Describing a group of objects mixed together with no apparent order or common factor.

Most classifications in social science have a <u>miscellaneous</u> category for bits of data which do not fit anywhere else.

xxviii) **remix** (v) (T)   ree-**miks**

In music, to mix and re-record elements of a track in a different way.

Modern digital technology enables DJs to <u>remix</u> old songs to make them more appealing to young **audiences**.

xxix) **miscible** (n) (u)   **mis**-uh-buh l

*Liquids that form a **homogeneous** mixture when added together.*

Oil and water are not <u>miscible</u>.

xxx) **miscegenation** (adj.)   mi-sej-*uh*-**ney**-sh*uh* n

Relationships or marriage between people of different racial groups.

<u>Miscegenation</u> was a common feature of some colonial societies.

Progression words
- miscible
- miscegenation

N.B.

Different spellings

Classical Latin borrowed extensively from the languages of other ancient civilizations including Old Italic (used in the Italian Peninsular prior to the Roman Empire), Phoenician (a North African empire) and Greek. However, some of the phonemes of these languages were difficult for Romans to pronounce and were written in different ways. Greek also used a different alphabet.

When Greek and Latin words first started to enter the English language in the early modern period, English did not have standard spelling or dictionaries. These did not arrive until the 18th century. In the Renaissance people even thought it was clever to spell their own name in different ways in different documents!

Hence the same Latin root can have different spellings in modern English, e.g. **hab/hib/habit** and **misc/mixt** in this unit. Bear this point in mind as you study subsequent lessons.

Study tip:

Even when you know the root of a word always check the English spelling in a dictionary, do not guess. To learn correct spellings try:

1. Phonic pronunciation
2. Copying out words in your notebook
3. Scrambled letter games

Vocabulary from Classical Roots

Section B: Unit 9, Lesson B – Common Verbs 4

1. here/hes (L)   "cling", "stick"

Core words

coherent

adhesion

inherent

i) **coherent** (adj.)   koh-**heer**-*uh* nt

Describing something in which the parts fit together to make a whole.

In university your tutors will expect you to produce <u>coherent</u> arguments in your essays and presentations.

ii) **adhesion** (n) (u)   ad-**hee**-zh*uh* n

The state of sticking to something.

Velcro is a material with good qualities of <u>adhesion</u> which is widely used to hold clothes together.

iii) **inherent** (adj.)   in-**heer**-*uh*nt

Describing something which is contained within and inseparable from the whole.

Despite the <u>inherent</u> risks, President Kennedy launched their Apollo program to put astronauts on the moon in 1961.

iv) **adherent** (n) (c)   ad-**heer**-*uh*nt

A follower of a religion or philosophy.

He was a charismatic leader with many <u>adherents</u>.

v) **hesitate** (v) (I)   **hez**-i-teyt

To pause for thought before making a decision. / To falter in the production of speech.

It is normal to <u>hesitate</u> to some extent when speaking in a foreign language.

Progression words

adherent

hesitate

2. jac/ject/ (L)   "throw"

Core words
- eject
- inject
- conjecture

vi) eject (v) (T)   ih-**jekt**

To forcibly remove a person from a place.

Rocket powered seats enable the pilots of modern fighter jets to eject from the cockpit in case of emergency.

vii) inject (v) (T)   in-**jekt**

To force a liquid into a crack, passage or cavity./To put a drug into a person's body using a Syringe.

Fracking works by injecting steam at high pressure into cracks in underground rocks to force out the oil.

viii) conjecture (n) (c), (v) (T)   k*uh*n-**jek**-cher

A guess or speculative statement. / To make a statement without solid evidence.

The CEO said media reports that he intended to resign were pure conjecture.

ix) projectile (n)(c)   pr*uh*-**jek**-tahyl

An object thrown or fired from a weapon.

The ancient Greeks and Romans did not have guns but they used huge catapults to fire large stones as projectiles to break down walls during sieges.

x) trajectory (n) (c)   tr*uh*-**jek**-t*uh*-ree

The course taken by an object in flight, usually a curve.

Ballistic **missiles** have a much higher trajectory than bullets.

Progression words
- projectile
- trajectory

162

3. caed/cid/caes/cis (L)   "cut", "kill"

Core words
- concise
- pesticide
- scissors

xi) **concise** (adj.)   k*uh*n-**sahys**

Describing something as briefly as possible.

Making writing more concise by cutting out repetition and waffle is an important academic skill.

xii) **pesticide** (n) (u)   **pes**-t*uh*-sahyd

A chemical which kills harmful plants or insects.

Using pesticides raises farmer's yields but can have unintended consequences for the ecosystem.

xiii) **scissors** (n) (plural)   **siz**-erz

A cutting tool with two blades.

Every home needs a good pair of scissors for opening bags in the kitchen and mending clothes.

xiv) **precise** (adj.)   pri-**sahys**

Exactness and accuracy of details or expression.

The police requested the witness to be precise about the timing of the accident.

xv) **incisive** (adj.)   in-**sahy**-siv

Describing something which cuts through confusion and gets to the heart of the matter.

Forming and asking incisive questions is the key skill of TV and newspaper interviewers.

Progression words
- precise
- incisive

4. sili/salt (L), alt (L) "jump", "high"

Core words
- assault
- desultory
- somersault

xvi) **assault** (v) (T), (n) (c) *uh*-**sawlt**

*To attack others. / An **incident** involving an attack on others.*

Jones was sentenced to 5 years in prison for a vicious assault on his colleague.

xvii) **desultory** (adj.) **des**-*uh* l-tawr-ee

Describing something inconsistent, lacking in energy or commitment.

Steve made only desultory attempts to revise for his exams, so it was no surprise when he failed.

xviii) **somersault** (v) (T), (n) (c) **suhm**-er-sawlt

A gymnastic movement in which the body makes a full rotation either forwards or backwards. / A complete reversal of a previously announced policy or decision.

Rhythmic gymnastics is a sport involving a series of **contortions** including somersaults made whilst using hoops or ribbons.

xix) **exalt** (v) (T) ig-**zawlt**

To praise someone. / To raise a person in rank or esteem.

The ancient Romans exalted successful generals with ceremonial parades through Rome with their booty.

xx) **resilience** (n) (u) ri-**zil**-y*uh* ns

The ability to bounce back after adversity.

The Canadian economy showed remarkable resilience after the global financial crisis in 2008.

Progression words
- exalt
- resilience

5. tribu (L)   "pay"

Core words

attribute

contribute

tribute

xxi) **attribute** (v) (T), (n) (c)   uh-**trib**-yoot (v); **a**-tr*uh*-byoot (n)

To acknowledge the source of something. To assign a cause to something. / A personal characteristic.

Climate scientists <u>attribute</u> most of the current rise in average temperatures to human activity.

xxii) **contribute** (v) (T)   k*uh*n-**trib**-yoot

To do or pay your share of some collective effort.

It is often alleged that internet companies fail to <u>contribute</u> their fair share of taxes in countries where they operate.

xxiii) **tribute** (n) (c)   **trib**-yoot

Praise for somebody. / A form of tax or gift paid in honour of somebody.

The Roman Empire required **subservient** peoples to pay tax in cash and as a <u>tribute</u> to the emperor who **conquered** them.

xxiv) **tribulation** (n) (c)   trib-y*uh*-**ley**-sh*uh*n

Serious trouble.

For many people in ancient Rome, just like today, the main cause of their <u>tribulations</u> was the need to pay bills or taxes.

xxv) **tributary** (n) (c)   **trib**-y*uh*-ter-ee

In geography, a river whose water flows into a larger river.

The many <u>tributaries</u> of the River Tiber brought water and transported goods and wealth to Rome.

Progression words

tribulation

tributary

6. vers/vert (L)   "turn"

xxvi) **advertise** (v) (T)   **ad**-ver-tahyz

Core words

advertise

adversity

controversy

To try to persuade people to buy a product or service.

Companies <u>advertise</u> in order to create awareness of a product, or turn public perceptions of it in a positive direction.

xxvii) **adversity** (n) (u)   ad-**vur**-si-tee

The condition of experiencing difficulties or bad luck.

Resilience in the face of <u>adversity</u> is an important success factor in academic study, business or sport.

xxviii) **controversy** (n) (c)   **kon**-tr*uh*-vur-see

The existence of disagreement about a topic among a large group of people.

Darwin's book "On the Origin of Species" caused huge <u>controversy</u> when it was first published in 1859.

xxix) **transverse** (adj.)   trans-**vurs**

In engineering, describing something mounted across an axis.

The Mini, designed by Alec Issigonis in 1959, was the first car to have a <u>transverse</u> engine mounted across the chassis.

xxx) **versatile** (adj.)   **vur**-s*uh*-tahyl

Describing something which can be used for several different purposes.

Progression words

transverse

versatile

Heraclides was an ancient Greek writer who was <u>versatile</u> enough to write about many different subjects.

N.B.

Multiple meanings

Root words, particularly verbs, can have a range of meanings in English. In this book space does not permit the listing of all possible meanings and the important point is to recognise the root and understand the derivation of the English word.

Study tip:

If you come across other meanings of a word in this book add example sentences to those included here. Note the context and try to understand the connection between the new word and the meaning of its root.

Vocabulary from Classical Roots

Section B: Unit 9, Exercises

Exercise 1: Jumbled letters

Unscramble the letters to make words from this unit.

1. tbihtaa ....
2. vtrsnaseer ....
3. eislecneri ....
4. pcdeities ....
5. vduncieoc ....
6. jlorecipte ....
7. udcudesoi ....
8. rtaenhed ....

Exercise 2: Crossword

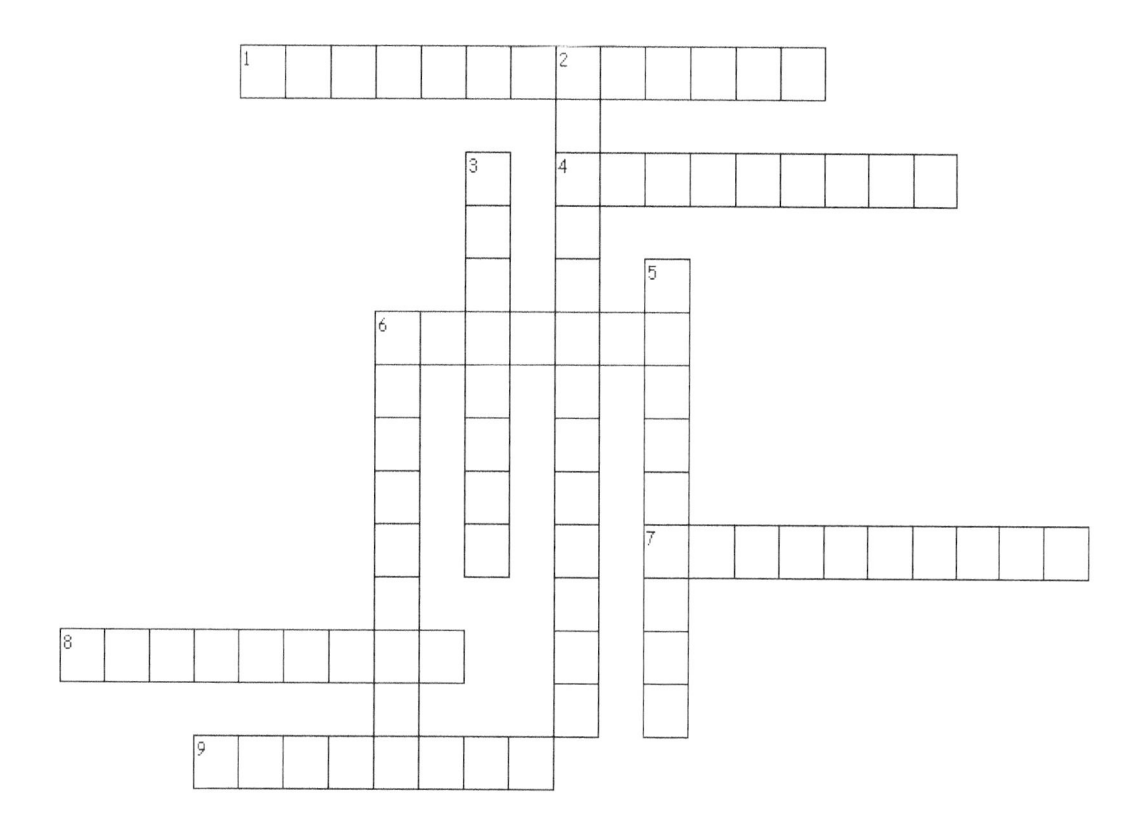

Across
1. A jumble of unconnected items
4. A river which flows into a larger one
6. Writing which has no extra words
7. The path taken by an object in flight
8. To reduce the seriousness of something
9. Describing something in which the parts fit together to make a whole

Down
2. A person's life story they write themselves
3. Two events happen at the same time
5. Something lacking in energy or commitment
6. A person who leads an orchestra

Exercise 3: Words used correctly or incorrectly

*Are the following sentences correct or incorrect? Write **C** or **I** in the brackets. If the sentence is incorrect, correct it. The first one has been done for you as an example.*

1. (I) If a law says that an activity is <u>prohibited,</u> that means it is <u>legal</u>.

    If a law says that an activity is prohibited, that means it is <u>illegal</u>.

2. (   ) An <u>authentic</u> tourism product is one which is a genuine reflection of the culture which produced it.

    ....

3. (   ) A <u>precise</u> set of directions enables one to reach the destination quickly.

    ....

4. (   ) To <u>deduce</u> a conclusion means to start with a theory and then find the evidence to prove it.

    ....

5. (   ) Fracking is an example of a process which relies on <u>ejecting</u> steam into a crack in underground rocks to force out the oil.

    ....

6. (   ) A person who is <u>level-headed</u> thinks clearly and logically and stays cool under pressure.

    ....

7. (   ) Immiscible is the opposite of <u>miscible.</u>

    ....

8. (   ) When prisons try to <u>rehabilitate</u> criminals they are trying to strengthen existing patterns of behaviour.

    ....

9. (   ) If a person has <u>leverage</u> in a situation, it means that they are unable to influence the outcome.

    ....

Section B: Unit 10, Lesson A – Adjectives, Qualities

1. acer (L), hed (L)   "bitter", "sweet"

Core words
- acrid
- acerbic
- acrimonious

i) **acrid** (adj.)   **ak**-rid

Describing something which has a strong and bitter taste in the mouth or nose.

The authorities urged people to keep doors and windows closed due to clouds of <u>acrid</u> smoke from the fire at a local tyre depot.

ii) **acerbic** (adj.)   uh-**sur**-bik

Describing something which is sour in taste. / Describing a person who is harsh in temperament or speech.

The office manager was unpopular because of her <u>acerbic</u> criticism of colleagues.

iii) **acrimonious** (adj.)   ak-r*uh*-**moh**-nee-*uh*s

Describing a bad-tempered argument or dispute.

Last night's televised debate between presidential candidates was often <u>acrimonious.</u>

iv) **exacerbate** (v) (T)   ek-s**as**-er-beyt

To make a situation worse.

The crisis in retailing caused by the switch to online shopping has been <u>exacerbated</u> by economic and political uncertainty.

v) **hedonism** (n) (u)   **heed**-n-iz-*uh*m

The belief that selfish pleasure is a way of life and a good thing.

Research has shown that <u>hedonism</u> is a major motive among consumers of luxury brands.

Progression words
- exacerbate
- hedonism

2. dyn (G) / fort (L)   "power", "strong"

Core words
- fortify
- fortitude
- dynamic

vi) fortify (v) (T)   **fawr**-t*uh*-fahy

To make strong to resist an attack or prepare for an ordeal.

The Roman Emperor Hadrian <u>fortified</u> the northern boundary of his empire by building a wall across northern England.

vii) fortitude (n) (u)   **fawr**-ti-tood

The quality of having mental strength in the face of adversity.

The British people showed great <u>fortitude</u> during the Battle of Britain and the Blitz in 1940-1941.

viii) dynamic (adj.)   dahy-**nam**-ik

The qualities of being driven, having energy and having the ability to get things done.

Many modern businesses believe that being <u>dynamic</u> is the best way to succeed in a difficult and uncertain business environment.

ix) dynamo (n) (c)   **dahy**-n*uh*-moh

A machine for generating electric current. / A person who produces a lot of energy.

The <u>dynamo</u> was invented by Michael Faraday in 1831.

x) forte (n) (c)   **fawr**-tey

A strong point in a person's personality or skill set.

She was appointed team leader because her <u>forte</u> is reaching **consensus**.

Progression words
- dynamo
- forte

3. gravis (L)   "heavy"

> **Core words**
>
> grave
>
> grief
>
> grievance

xi) **grave** (adj.), (n) (c)   greyv

Describing something which is serious or tragic. / A hole in the ground dug to bury a dead body.

The early 5th century CE was a grave time for the Roman Empire as Italy was overrun by the Goths and Rome was **conquered** in 410 AD.

xii) **grief** (n) (u)   greef

A feeling of loss or sadness.

Dogs and cats as well as humans feel grief when someone close to them passes away.

xiii) **grievance** (n) (c)   **gree**-v*uh*ns

An issue a person has with others when they feel they have been wronged in some way.

Workers sometimes go on strike to force management to address their grievances.

xiv) **aggravate** (v) (T)   **ag**-r*uh*-veyt

*To make a situation worse (synonym of **exacerbate**).*

In law, judges may increase a criminal's sentence if there are circumstances which aggravate his/her crime.

xv) **gravitate** (v) (T)   **grav**-i-teyt

The action of pulling something towards another person or object.

All over the world ambitious young people gravitate from the countryside to the big **dynamic** cities.

> **Progression words**
>
> aggravate
>
> gravitate

173

4. pugn/a/(L), pung (L)   "fight"

Core words
- pungent
- pugnacious
- repugnant

xvi) **pungent** (adj.)   **puhn**-j*uh*nt

*Describing a sharp, biting or caustic taste or smell, (synonym of **acrid**).*

Cordite used in artillery shells has a distinctive <u>pungent</u> smell.

xvii) **pugnacious** (adj.)   puhg-**ney**-sh*uh*s

Describing somebody who wants to fight.

Army recruiting posters often show a man with a <u>pugnacious</u> expression.

xviii) **repugnant** (adj.)   ri-**puhg**-n*uh*nt

Something which makes a negative impression on your senses. / Something which is contrary to your values.

Some people find the idea of using live animals in medical research <u>repugnant</u>.

xix) **pugilism** (n) (u)   **pyoo**-j*uh*-liz-*uh*m

An old-fashioned name for the sport of boxing.

The ancient Greek Olympic Games did not include <u>pugilism</u> in its **contemporary** form but did feature a kind of wrestling in which punching was allowed.

xx) **impugn** (v) (T)   im-**pyoon**

To cast doubt on another person's integrity.

In the ancient world if a man's honour was <u>impugned</u> he was expected to fight to defend himself.

Progression words
- pugilism
- impugn

174

5. soph (G) "wise"

Core words
- philosopher
- sophisticated
- sophomore

xxi) philosopher (n) (c)   fi-**los**-*uh*-fer

A thinker, someone who studies the principles of knowledge, ethics, etc.

A Greek philosopher and playwright, Sophocles, gave his name to the root *soph* and thus, to his profession.

xxii) sophisticated (adj.)   suh-**fis**-ti-key-tid

Describing someone whose ideas have been changed by education or experience so that they are no longer naïve.

The internet is making shoppers more and more sophisticated.

xxiii) sophomore (n) (c)   **sof**-*uh*-mawr

A second-year student in high school or university.

Sophomores are generally expected to have more knowledge and wisdom than freshmen.

xxiv) sophistry (n) (u)   **sof**-*uh*-stree

An attempt to fool somebody by using clever but false arguments.

Political populism is a rejection of what its supporters see as the sophistry of the establishment.

xxv) Sophists (n) (c)   **sof**-ist

Orators in ancient Greece and the Middle Ages who could be hired to come up with spurious arguments in favour of anything.

The Protestant Reformation was in large part a reaction against the pedantic theology of the medieval Sophists.

Progression words
- sophistry
- Sophists

175

6. vac (L)   "empty"

Core words
- vacant
- vacation
- evacuate

xxvi) **vacant** (adj.)   **vey**-k*uh* nt

Describing a place or position which is not occupied.

Hotel managers try to keep the number of <u>vacant</u> rooms to a minimum and employers try to keep the number of <u>vacant</u> positions to a minimum.

xxvii) **vacation** (n) (c)   vey-**key**-sh*uh* n

A holiday; literally, a time empty of work.

In most western countries full-time employees have a legal right to some paid <u>vacation</u> every year.

xxviii) **evacuate** (v) (T)   ih-**vak**-yoo-eyt

To remove people from a place of danger.

It is now routine for areas of the American south-east to be <u>evacuated</u> before they are hit by hurricanes.

xxix) **vacuum** (n) (c)   **vak**-yoom

In physics, a space empty of matter.

Life cannot exist in a <u>vacuum</u> because there is no oxygen.

xxx) **vacuous** (adj.)   **vak**-yoo-*uh* s

Describing an argument which is empty of content or logic.

In critical thinking classes students are taught to avoid writing <u>vacuous</u> sentences.

Progression words
- vacuum
- vacuous

N.B.

Synonyms

In the past English sometimes formed words from more than one root with the same or similar meanings. Sometimes this would be one Greek and one Latin root. On other occasions two roots from the same language were borrowed. This results in the creation of synonyms in English.

Examples

acer (L)   acrid   pung (L)   pungent

Both describe something sharp, bitter or caustic.

acer (L)   exacerbate   grav (L)   aggravate

Both mean to make something worse.

However, be careful with collocations. We tend to say acrid smoke but a pungent smell.

Study tip:

Make notes of synonyms like this to increase your vocabulary range and help avoid repetition.

Vocabulary from Classical Roots

Section B: Unit 10, Lesson B – Similarities and Differences

1. ambi (L)   "both", "on both/all sides"

Core words
ambiguous
ambient
ambience

i) **ambiguous** (adj.)   am-**big**-yoo-*uh*s

Describing a message which can be understood in more than one way.

Students complained that the last question in their English literature examination was ambiguous.

ii) **ambient** (adj.)   **am**-bee-*uh* nt

Describing something related to the surrounding area or the environment.

The ambient (air) temperature on the mountain top in summer was below freezing.

iii) **ambience** (n) (u)   **am**-bee-*uh* ns

The surroundings and atmosphere of a place.

The new restaurant has a relaxed and welcoming ambience.

iv) **ambidextrous** (adj.)   am-bi-**dek**-str*uh* s

Describing a person who can use both hands with equal skill.

Being ambidextrous is a very useful skill for mechanics.

v) **ambivalent** (n) (u)   am-**biv**-*uh*-l*uh* nt

The condition of being undecided. / The condition of having mixed feelings about a topic.

Studies show that many people are ambivalent about the claimed future benefits of automation in the home.

Progression words
ambidextrous
ambivalent

2. equ (L) "equal", "even", "level"

Core words
- equality
- equator
- equivalent

vi) equality (n) (u)   ih-**kwol**-i-tee

The condition of being equal in status or wealth. / The condition of having equal rights.

Some governments believe that there should be greater <u>equality</u> in society.

vii) equator (n) (u)   ih-**kwey**-ter

An imaginary line which divides the world into two equal halves called hemispheres.

The <u>equator</u> runs through hot countries such as Brazil, the Democratic Republic of Congo and Indonesia.

viii) equivalent (adj.), (n) (c)   ih-**kwiv**-*uh*-*luh* nt

Something which is equal to or similar to something else.

If goods bought in a shop are faulty, then customers are entitled to a refund or goods of an <u>equivalent</u> value.

ix) equilibrium (adj.)   ee-kw*uh*-**lib**-ree-*uh*m

A value at which two or more items are in balance.

Many people, nowadays, struggle to find <u>equilibrium</u> between work and family life.

x) equivocal (adj.)   ih-**kwiv**-*uh*-kuh l

Describing a statement which can have several meanings, all of them equally likely to be correct.

In court, the defendant's explanations for his behaviour were always <u>equivocal</u> and the jury found him guilty.

Progression words
- equilibrium
- equivocal

Vocabulary from Classical Roots

3. idi (G)   "own", "personal", "unique"

> **Core words**
> identical
> identify
> idiot

xi) **identical** (adj.)   ahy-**den**-ti-k*uh*l

Describing two or more objects which are precisely the same.

Occasionally pairs of <u>identical</u> twins are born.

xii) **identify** (v) (T)   ih-**den**-t*uh*-fahy

To recognise something as belonging to a known group of objects or persons.

Computer systems are being developed which can <u>identify</u> human faces to provide security checks in buildings.

xiii) **idiot** (n) (c)   **id**-ee-*uh*t   *

A very silly or stupid person.

Calling somebody an <u>idiot</u> is a very common insult but often reflects a failure to engage with their ideas.

xiv) **idiosyncrasy** (n) (c)   id-ee-*uh*-**sing**-kr*uh*-see

A personal habit, or mannerism often unique to a person.

J.K. Rowling, author of the Harry Potter stories, has an <u>idiosyncrasy</u>: she likes to write in cafes.

xv) **idiomatic** (adj.)   id-ee-*uh*-**mat**-ik

Speech patterns which are peculiar to a particular language or dialect.

<u>Idiomatic</u> speech is one of the hardest things for learners of a foreign language to acquire.

> **Progression words**
> idiosyncrasy
> idiomatic

4. is/iso (G), insula (L)   "the same", "island"

Core words
- isotope
- isosceles
- isolated

xvi) **isotope** (n) (c)   ahy-s*uh*-tohp

In chemistry, two or more forms of an element with the same number of protons but different numbers of neutrons and therefore, different atomic weights.

Understanding the differences between isotopes of uranium is crucial to understanding the arguments about proliferation of nuclear power stations and weapons.

xvii) **isosceles** (adj.)   ahy-**sos**-*uh*-leez

Describing a triangle with two angles and sides the same.

The theory of the isosceles triangle was developed in ancient Greece but nobody knows by whom.

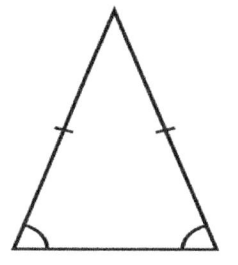

xviii) **isolated** (adj.)   **ahy**-s*uh*-ley-tid

Describing something or someone that is separate, alone or different from others.

He grew up in an isolated village.

xix) **isotonic** (adj.)   ahy-s*uh*-**ton**-ik

Related to a liquid having same concentration as body fluid.

Athletes use isotonic drinks to replace bodily fluids lost in sweat during vigorous exercise.

xx) **isometric** (adj.)   ahy-s*uh*-**me**-trik

Describing something which has equal measures.

In math, an isometric cube has three sides that are all of equal length.

Progression words
- isotonic
- isometric

Vocabulary from Classical Roots

5. syl/sym/syn (G) "together", "with", "the same"

Core words
- synonym
- symmetrical
- synergy

xxi) **synonym** (n) (c) **sin**-*uh*-nim

A word with the same or similar meaning as another.

Using a range of synonyms can make your writing much more interesting.

xxii) **symmetrical** (n) (u) si-**me**-trikl

Describing a situation in which two sides of an object are similar in shape, size, colour, etc.

Ancient Greek temples were usually designed to be symmetrical.

xxiii) **synergy** (n) (c) **sin**-er-jee

A situation in which elements combine to form more than the sum of their parts.

Businesses considering a partnership or merger look for synergies which will make the combined company stronger than the two separate entities.

xxiv) **syllogism** (n) (c) **sil**-*uh*-jiz-*uh*m

In critical thinking, an argument and conclusion supported by two premises.

Syllogisms are commonly presented in the form of arguments such as, all A is C; all B is A; therefore, all B is C.

xxv) **synchronous** (adj.) **sing**-kr*uh*-n*uh*s

Describing two or more events which occur at the same time, cf. ***asynchronous*** *(Unit 3).*

A phone call is an example of synchronous communication because both speakers have to be present at the same time.

Progression words
- syllogism
- synchronous

6. vari (L)   "vary"

Core words
- various
- invariable
- variety

xxvi) **various** (adj.)   **vair**-ee-*uh*s

Describing objects which differ in a number of ways.

Popular music can be divided into <u>various</u> styles such as pop, heavy metal, R&B, house, rap, etc.

xxvii) **invariably** (adv.)   in-**vair**-ee-*uh*-b*uh*li

Describing something which happens every time, without exception.

History shows that major changes in the earth's climate <u>invariably</u> cause mass extinction of species.

xxviii) **variety** (n) (c)   v*uh*-**rahy**-i-tee

The state of something being diverse.

The Tate modern Art Gallery in London **exhibits** a huge <u>variety</u> of styles of art.

xxix) **variance** (n) (c)   **vair**-ee-*uh* ns

In accounting and statistics, the difference between an expected value and an actual value.

Management accountants monitor <u>variances</u> to ensure compliance with departmental budgets.

xxx) **variegate** (v) (T)   **vair**-ee-i-geyt

To increase the variety of something.

Nowadays cities have had to <u>variegate</u> their range of attractions to appeal to a wider range of potential tourists.

Progression words
- variance
- variegate

N.B.

Visual Decoding Skills

Visual decoding skills are a collection of tools and methods you can use to work out the meaning of new words you encounter in academic reading and listening. They are a synthesis of the properties of roots and study techniques we have learned in this book, i.e.

i) the meaning of the root

ii) the meaning of prefixes, e.g. negatives

iii) the meaning of suffixes, e.g. part of speech, person, academic subject, belief, etc.

iv) the context of the sentence where context includes the topic and the words before, or after the new word.

v) any definition given in the text by the author.

vi) any examples given in the text.

vii) any pictures or diagrams given in the text.

Study tip:

When you find a new word in reading, do not go straight to your dictionary, try to use the visual decoding skills given above to **deduce** the meaning, then check your dictionary to see if you are right. Finally make a note of the new word including the part of speech, the context and any collocations.

Chains of Reasoning

xiii) **idiot:** The ancient world had a very different understanding of mental conditions to that prevailing today. For example, lack of intelligence was not considered to be caused by genetics or mental illness in general but was considered to be a personal attribute. This meant that the sufferer was considered to be responsible for their condition and they were often **denigrated** in a way which is now offensive.

Section B: Unit 10, Exercises

Exercise 1: Visual decoding skills 1: word formation

Choose the best answer for each question below.

1. (   ) The root in the word *equator* means:

    a) unique   b) equal   c) various   d) wise

2. (   ) The suffix in the word *fortifications* tells you the word is a .... having something to do with strength:

    a) noun   b) verb   c) adjective   d) adverb

3. (   ) The root in the word *synthesis* means:

    a) alone   b) both   c) heavy   d) together

4. (   ) The prefix in the word *disequilibrium* means:

    a) all   b) not   d) bad   d) one

5. (   ) The root in the word *dynamite* means:

    a) electric   b) fight   c) power   d) bitter

6) (   ) The suffix in the word *hedonistic* tells you that it is an .... having something to do with selfish pleasure:

    a) verb   b) noun   c) adverb   d) adjective

7. (   ) By using the prefix and the root you can deduce that the word *inequality* is talking about:

    a) something that is equally shared   b) something that does not vary
    c) something that is not personal   d) something that is not equally shared

8. (   ) By using the root you can deduce that the process of *vacuum forming* in the manufacture of thin plastic objects involves:

    a) a space full of air   b) a shape with two sides the same
    c) a space empty of air   d) a process which makes a caustic smell

Vocabulary from Classical Roots

Exercise 2: Visual decoding skills 2: context and collocations

Choose the best answer for each question below.

1. (   ) In which context are you likely to encounter the word *isotope*?

    a) weather forecasting   b) nuclear physics   c) engineering   d) business

2. (   ) In which context are you likely to encounter the word *isosceles*?

    a) business   b) chemistry   c) geometry   d) military history

3. (   ) Which of the following words collocates with *debate* to describe a bad-tempered argument?

    a) ambivalent   b) sophistry   c) syllogism   d) acrimonious

4. (   ) In which context are you most likely to encounter the word *synergy?*

    a) business   b) ancient history   c) math   d) physics

5. (   ) Which of the following words might collocate with *lively* to describe a bar in a holiday brochure for teenagers?

    a) ambiguous   b) ambience   c) vacuous   d) grave

6. (   ) In which context are you likely to encounter the word *idiosyncrasy*?

    a) a description of a business   b) a description of a manufacturing process

    c) a description of a building   d) a description of a personality

7. (   ) Which of the following words sometimes collocates with *twins*?

    a) identical   b) idiomatic   c) various   d) equivalent

8. (   ) In which of the following contexts might you have to calculate *variances*?

    a) literature   b) computing   c) accounting   d) nuclear physics

Vocabulary from Classical Roots

Exercise 3: Visual decoding skills 3: definitions and examples

Choose the best answer for each question below.

1. (   ) Which word can be defined as "the distinguishing character or personality of an individual"?

    a) idiot   b) identity   c) identical   d) sophisticated

2. (   ) The sentence, "All men are mortal, Sophocles was a man, therefore Sophocles was mortal" is an example of .... :

    a) a variance   b) ambiguity   c) a syllogism   d) a synonym

3. (   ) "In economics, when supply and demand are in balance prices will be stable." This sentence is an example of a state of .... :

    a) equilibrium   b) variance   c) pugilism   d) equality

4. (   ) Which of the following words can be defined as "action to broaden the range of something such as products sold in a supermarket"?

    a) gravitate   b) variegate   c) evacuate   d) aggravate

5. (   ) Which of the following does the word *vacant* not collocate with?

    a) expression   b) room   c) position   d) triangle

6. (   ) Which of the following words collocates with *student* to describe a person in his/her second year of studies?

    a) sophomore   b) wise   c) sophisticated   d) vacuous

7. (   ) Which word can be defined as "having the ability to use the left hand and right hand with equal skill"?

    a) ambiguous   b) asynchronous   c) ambidextrous   d) aggravating

8. (   ) Which of the following words can be collocated with *cause* to describe a chain of events which always occur?

    a) asymmetrically   b) unequivocally   d) idiotically   d) invariably

Vocabulary from Classical Roots

Consolidation 2 – Units 1-10

Activity A: Countable and uncountable nouns

One of the biggest difficulties faced by students when learning to use new academic vocabulary is the question of countable and uncountable nouns. The problem is that whether a noun is countable or uncountable determines the grammar of the rest of the sentence, i.e. agreements with verbs, referring pronouns, etc.

There are some rules you can learn to help you based on categories of nouns. Remember that the Greek and Latin suffixes we have learned in this book can sometimes help you recognise the category a word belongs to.

The following table is a guide. Use it to help you understand which types of nouns are countable and uncountable and add your own examples as you review the book.

Category	Countable (c) / uncountable (u)	Example	Your examples
academic subjects	u	cardiology	
buildings/ rooms	c	auditorium	
countries, continents	u	Mesopotamia	
diseases/medical conditions	u	cirrhosis	
elements	u	chromium	
physical forces	u	vacuum	
gases	u	chlorine	
ideas, beliefs	u	claustrophobia	
machines	c	dynamo	

Vocabulary from Classical Roots

people (experts, followers, etc.)	c	dermatologist
processes, practices	u	immigration
scientific instruments	c	micrometre
shapes	c	isosceles triangle
states of mind	u	apathy

Activity B: Alphabetical vocabulary review

Fill in the missing words by using the definitions given below. The first letter and unit in which the word first appeared are given to help you.

Example:

A	Departure from the normal standards of behaviour (Unit 5)	*Aberration*
A	An adjective describing care given before birth (Unit 3)	....
B	A person who loves books (Unit 6)	....
C	A greenish gas once used as an anaesthetic (Unit 7)	....
D	A type of tree which sheds its leaves every autumn (Unit 9)	....
E	An imaginary line dividing the world into two hemispheres (Unit 10)	....
F	An adjective describing something which bends easily (Unit 2)	....
G	An adjective describing old people (Unit 4)	....
H	A medical condition involving extreme stress (Unit 2)	....
I	To make something worse or more difficult (Unit 5)	....
J	A term for a young person usually used in the legal system (Unit 4)	....
K	A unit of measure for electricity (Unit 1)	....
L	A formal word for a railway engine (Unit 7)	....
M	Describing a bird or animal which moves between habitats (Unit 8)	....
N	Describing the skill of being good with figures (Unit 1)	....
O	A branch of dentistry concerned with the shape of the teeth (Unit 4)	....
P	A chemical intended to kill insects or plants (Unit 9)	....
Q	A geometrical shape with four sides (Unit 1)	....
R	A person who betrays an idea, a club or a country (Unit 5)	....
S	To put something under the surface of a liquid such as water (Unit 3)	....

Vocabulary from Classical Roots

T	The flight path of an object such as a missile through the air (Unit 9)	....
U	A word to describe a decision or action taken by one party alone (Unit 1)	....
V	The extent to which things can be seen (Unit 6)	....

Activity C: Writing

Choose a controversial topic in your country or culture and write a critical analysis of the arguments used by both sides. Use as many of the critical thinking and persuasive words in the Word-bank below as you can.

Word-bank

abstain	abhorrent	advocate	aggravate	alleviate
antagonist	apathy	coincide	concur	concise
conform	consensus	contradict	deduce	dismiss
impugn	inquiry	irrational	negativity	obstruct
oppose	opposition	proponent	propose	proposition

Vocabulary from Classical Roots

Section C – (i)   Answers to Exercises

Unit 1

Exercise 1: Sentence completion

1. triangle	2. decibels	3. unified	4. centigrade	5. numerate
6. binary	7. quintessence	8. monotheist	9. university	10. kilowatts

Exercise 2: Crossword

Across

3. binomial	7. decade	8. pentathlon	9. monoplane

Down

1. quadruple	2. centenary	4. numerous	5. multilateral
6. decimate	9. monarch		

Exercise 3: Multiple Choice

1. b	2. d	3. a	4. c
5. c	6. d	7. a	8. c

Unit 2

Exercise 1: Root words used correctly or incorrectly

1. Correct

2. Incorrect: A microchip is a very <u>small</u> electronic circuit at the heart of a computer.

3. Incorrect: Steel is a very <u>inflexible</u> material used for making car bodies.

4. Correct

5. Incorrect: Newspaper <u>circulations</u> are dropping dramatically and some titles are now available online only.

6. Correct

7. Correct

8. Incorrect: Children who <u>are hyperactive / have ADHD</u> have too much energy and are often disruptive in school.

Exercise 2: Scales

1.
   a) oval
   b) trigonometry
   c) rectangle
   d) polygon
   e) hexagon
   f) octagon

2.
   a) micro
   b) mini
   c) medi
   d) macro
   e) hyper
   f) ultra

Vocabulary from Classical Roots

Exercise 3: Fill in the Blanks

(1) circulates (2) ultramodern (3) scans (4) globulins

(5) hypertension (6) microbiology (7) microscopic (8) hyperventilation

Unit 3

Exercise 1: Antonyms and collocations

1 (a) 2 (c) 3 (b) 4 (d)

5 (c) 6 (a) 7 (d) 8 (b)

Exercise 2: Jumbled letters

1. superfluous 2. antenatal 3. precedent 4. telecommuting

5. transport 6. intersection 7. subjunctive 8. intravenous

Exercise 3: Matching definitions

1 = e 2 = c 3 = g 4 = b

5 = d 6 = h 7 = a 8 = f

Unit 4

Exercise 1: Matching roots and suffixes

| 1. geriatric | 2. paediatric | 3. physics | 4. orthodontics | 5. ……..path |
| 6. ……… gram | 7. physician | 8. pedestrian | 9. optician | 10. paediatrician |

Answers 1-4 and answers 7-10 can be in any order.

Exercise 2: Fill in the Blanks

1. (ante) natal   2. maternity   3. maternal   4. paediatricians   5. juvenile

6. matrimony   7. mortality   8. geriatric   9. immortal

Exercise 3: Collocations

1. paternity leave   2. fraternal greetings   3. oral English

4. heterodox beliefs   5. pedestrian pace   6. nascent movement

7. matriarchal society   8. manual job   9. neurotic behaviour

Unit 5

Exercise 1: Matching prefixes and endings

ab	anti	bene	contra	im	prob
abstain	antipathy	beneficial	contravene	immobile	probability
abnormal	antidote	benefactor	contradict	implausible	probation

Exercise 2: Collocations and register

1. b 2. c 3. a 4. d
5. c 6. c 7. b 8. d

Vocabulary from Classical Roots

Exercise 3: Word search

G	B	E	G	A	J	H	A	I	C	D	U	R	K	A
B	T	Z	H	M	B	W	T	V	F	F	U	E	R	N
Y	I	N	P	P	C	E	J	D	L	B	F	N	M	T
V	V	A	E	J	G	D	R	E	T	W	G	E	E	A
Z	I	U	V	L	Q	A	L	R	P	J	D	G	M	G
R	U	I	A	Y	O	E	C	K	A	E	M	A	Y	O
T	O	L	F	W	K	V	G	O	T	T	U	D	T	N
C	O	N	T	R	E	T	E	M	P	S	I	E	U	I
Q	V	O	H	P	S	U	F	N	F	Y	R	O	I	S
H	K	K	C	V	G	R	T	L	E	Z	B	C	N	T
C	Y	F	M	E	L	Q	M	M	U	B	O	W	D	L
E	T	A	C	I	D	U	J	D	A	D	R	L	T	Z
D	Y	S	P	E	P	S	I	A	Y	F	P	O	Q	X
U	K	P	R	O	Z	E	B	O	R	P	P	J	F	S
R	H	U	K	P	N	C	P	X	J	S	O	Q	D	N

Consolidation 1 – Units 1-5
Activity A: Building your own word-bank

Verb	Noun (s)	Adjective (s)
predict	a) *object:* prediction	a) *positive:* predictable
	b) *agent:* predictor	b) *negative:* unpredictable
supervise	supervisor	supervisory
telescope	**telescope**	telescopic
xxxxxxxxxxxxxxxxxxxx	a) *subject:* psychology	psychological
	b) *person:* **psychologist**	
manufacture	manufacturer	a) *state:* manufactured
		b) *process:* manufacturing
patronise	a) *person:* patron	a) *condition:* patronised
	b) *practice:* **patronage**	b) *behaviour*: **patronising**
contradict	contradiction	contradictory
connect	**connector**	a) *positive*: well connected
		b) negative: **badly connected**
a) *positive:* **approve**	a) *positive:* approval	a) *state of mind:* approving
b) *negative:* disapprove	b) *negative:* disapproval	b) *condition:* approved
a) *positive:* propose	a) person: opponent	opposite
b) *negative:* oppose	b) opinion: **opposition**	

Vocabulary from Classical Roots

Unit 6

Exercise 1: Synonyms and antonyms

1. d   2. c   3. a   4. b
5. c   6. a   7. c

Exercise 2: Crossword

Across

5. intact   6. deodorant   8. egotistical   9. phonology

10. philharmonic

Down

1. resent   2. pathetic   3. advocate   4. audition

7. enamour

Exercise 3: Sentence completion (collocations)

1. sympathetically   2. odourless   3. audiences   4. hostilities
5. video   6. egocentric   7. vocabulary   8. vistas

Unit 7

Exercise 1: Matching pictures

a) reporter   b) helicopter   c) aureole   d) aerosol

e) locomotive   f) Argentina   g) rhododendron   h) melanoma

i) cyclone   j) port

Exercise 2: Collocations, context and synonyms

1. d	2. b	3. a	4. b + c
5. d	6. a	7. b	8. c

Exercise 3: Fill in the Blanks

1. navigate	2. ports	3. exports	4. locomotive
5. tricycles	6. automobile	7. commuting	8. astronauts

Unit 8

Exercise 1: Completing a context table

1. engineering
2. personality
3. retort
4. structure
5. infrastructure
6. introspective
7. construe
8. exports
9. torsion
10. circumspect

Exercise 2: Matching definitions

1. j
2. d
3. g
4. h
5. b
6. c
7. a
8. i
9. e
10. f

Exercise 3: Collocations

1. extort money
2. witty retort
3. public inquiry
4. conquer a country
5. conserve energy
6. free admission
7. attract attention
8. spectator sport
9. chemical formula
10. voluntary work

Vocabulary from Classical Roots

Unit 9

Exercise 1: Scrambled letters

1. habitat
2. transverse
3. resilience
4. pesticide
5. conducive
6. projectile
7. deciduous
8. adherent

Exercise 2: Crossword

Across

1. miscellaneous
4. tributary
6. concise
7. trajectory
8. alleviate
9. coherent

Down

2. autobiography
3. coincide
5. desultory
6. conductor

Exercise 3: Words used correctly and incorrectly

2. correct

3. correct

4. To deduce a conclusion means to start with the evidence and reason from it.

5. Fracking is an example of a process which relies on injecting steam into a crack in underground rocks to force out the oil.

6. correct

7. correct

8. When prisons try to rehabilitate criminals they are trying to change existing patterns of behaviour.

9. If a person has leverage in a situation, it means that they are able to influence the outcome.

Unit 10

Exercise 1: Visual decoding skills 1, word formation

| 1. b | 2. a | 3. d | 4. b |
| 5. c | 6. d | 7. d | 8. c |

Exercise 2: Visual decoding skills 2, context and collocations

| 1. b | 2. c | 3. d | 4. a |
| 5. b | 6. d | 7. a | 8. c |

Exercise 3: Visual decoding skills 3, definitions and examples

| 1. b | 2. c | 3. a | 4. b |
| 5. d | 6. a | 7. c | 8. d |

Consolidation 2 – Units 1-10

Activity A. Alphabetical vocabulary review

A. antenatal	B. bibliophile	C. chloroform	D. deciduous
E. equator	F. flexible	G. geriatric	H. hypertension
I. impair	J. juvenile	K. kilowatt	L. locomotive
M. migratory	N. numerate	O. orthodontics	P. pesticide
Q. quadrilateral	R. renegade	S. submerge	T. trajectory
U. unilateral	V. visibility		

Section C (ii) – Wordlist

A

aberration (n) (c)	Unit 5 Lesson A
abhorrent (adj.)	Unit 5 Lesson A
abnormal (adj.)	Unit 5 Lesson A
abnegate (v) (T)	Unit 5 Lesson B
abstain (v) (T) (I)	Unit 5 Lesson A
adjudicate (v) (T)	Unit 5 Lesson A
accident (n) (c)	Unit 9 Lesson A
acerbic (adj.)	Unit 10 Lesson A
acrid (adj.)	Unit 10 Lesson A
acrimonious (adj.)	Unit 10 Lesson A
acrophobia (n) (u)	Unit 6 lesson B
adherent (n) (c)	Unit 9 lesson B
adhesion (n) (u)	Unit 9 Lesson B
admission (n) (c)	Unit 8 Lesson B
adversity (n) (u)	Unit 9 Lesson B
advertise (v) (T)	Unit 9 Lesson B
advocate (v) (T)	Unit 6 Lesson A
aerate (v) (T)	Unit 7 Lesson B
aerodynamics (n) (u)	Unit 7 Lesson B
aeroelastic (n)	Unit 7 Lesson B
aerospace (n) (c) (adj.)	Unit 7 Lesson B
aerosol (n) (c)	Unit 7 Lesson B
aggravate (v) (T)	Unit 10 Lesson A
albino (adj.)	Unit 7 Lesson A
alignment (n) (c)	Unit 2 Lesson A
alleviate (v) (T)	Unit 9 Lesson A
alter ego (n) (u)	Unit 6 Lesson B
ambidextrous (adj.)	Unit 10 Lesson B
ambience (n) (u)	Unit 10 lesson B
ambient (adj.)	Unit 10 Lesson B
ambiguous (adj.)	Unit 10 Lesson B
ambivalent (adj.)	Unit 10 Lesson B
amorously (adv.)	Unit 6 Lesson B
amenity (n) (c)	Unit 6 Lesson B
amicably (adv.)	Unit 6 Lesson B
amity (n) (u)	Unit 6 Lesson B
anachronism (n) (c)	Unit 3 Lesson A
android (n) (c)	Unit 4 Lesson B
androgynous (adj.)	Unit 4 Lesson B
annul (v) (T)	Unit 1 Lesson B
antagonist (n) (c)	Unit 5 Lesson A
antecedent (n) (c)	Unit 3 Lesson A
antediluvian (adj.)	Unit 3 Lesson A
antemeridian (adj.)	Unit 3 Lesson A
antenatal (adj.)	Unit 3 Lesson A
anteroom (n) (c)	Unit 3 Lesson A
antics (n) (plural)	Unit 5 Lesson A
antipathy (n) (c)	Unit 5 Lesson A
anti-retroviral (adj.)	Unit 3 Lesson A
antidote (n) (c)	Unit 5 Lesson A
antisocial (adj.)	Unit 5 Lesson A
apathy (n) (u)	Unit 6 Lesson B
approbation (n) (u)	Unit 5 Lesson B
approve (v) (T) (I)	Unit 5 Lesson A
arachnophobia (n) (u)	Unit 6 Lesson B
Argentina (n) (u)	Unit 7 Lesson A
aspirin (n) (u)	Unit 7 Lesson A
assault (v) (T) (n) (c)	Unit 9 Lesson B
assent (v) (T) (n) (c)	Unit 6 Lesson B
astronaut (n) (c)	Unit 7 Lesson B
asynchronous (adj.)	Unit 3 Lesson A
attribute (n) (c) (v) (T)	Unit 9 Lesson B
audible (adj.)	Unit 6 Lesson A
audience (n) (c)	Unit 6 Lesson A
audio visual (adj.)	Unit 6 Lesson A
audition (n) (c)	Unit 6 Lesson A
auditorium (n) (c)	Unit 6 Lesson A
aura (n) (c)	Unit 7 Lesson A
aureole (n) (c)	Unit 7 Lesson A
autarky (n) (c)	Unit 9 Lesson A
authentic (adj.)	Unit 9 Lesson A
autobiography (n) (c)	Unit 9 Lesson A
automatic (adj.)	Unit 9 Lesson A
automation (n) (u)	Unit 9 Lesson A

Vocabulary from Classical Roots

automobile (n) (c)	Unit 7 Lesson B	chrysalis (n) (c)	Unit 7 Lesson A
autopsy (n) (c)	Unit 4 Lesson A	chrysanthemum (n) (c)	Unit 7 Lesson A
aversion (n) (c)	Unit 5 Lesson A	circulate (v) (T)	Unit 2 Lesson A
		circulation (n) (c)	Unit 2 Lesson A
B		circumspect (adj.)	Unit 8 Lesson A
		circumstances (n)	Unit 2 Lesson A
benefit (n) (c) (v) (T)	Unit 5 Lesson B	circumvent (v) (T)	Unit 16 Lesson A
benefactor (n) (c)	Unit 5 Lesson B	circus (n) (c)	Unit 2 Lesson A
beneficial (adj.)	Unit 5 Lesson B	cirrhosis (n) (u)	Unit 7 Lesson A
benevolent (adj.)	Unit 5 Lesson B	claustrophobia (n) (u)	Unit 6 Lesson B
benign (adj.)	Unit 5 Lesson B	coherent (adj.)	Unit 9 Lesson B
bibliophile (n) (c)	Unit 6 Lesson B	coincide (v) (T)	Unit 9 Lesson A
bicycle (n) (c)	Unit 1 Lesson A	collaborate (v) (T)	Unit 11 Lesson B
bimonthly (adj.)	Unit 1 Lesson A	Colorado (n) (u)	Unit 7 Lesson A
binary (adj.)	Unit 1 Lesson A	commute (v) (T)	Unit 7 Lesson B
binoculars (n) (u)	Unit 1 Lesson A	compassion (adj.)	Unit 8 Lesson a
binomial (adj.)	Unit 1 Lesson A	concise (adj.)	Unit 9 Lesson B
		conducive (adj.)	Unit 9 Lesson A
		conductor (n) (c)	Unit 9 Lesson A
C		conform (v) (T)	Unit 8 Lesson A
		conjecture (n) (u) (v) (T)	Unit 9 Lesson B
cacophony (n) (c)	Unit 6 Lesson A	conquer (v) (T)	Unit 8 Lesson B
cadaver (n) (c)	Unit 9 Lesson A	consensus (n) (u)	Unit 6 Lesson B
capture (v) (T)	Unit 8 Lesson B	conserve (v) (T)	Unit 8 Lesson B
captivate (v) (T)	Unit 8 Lesson B	conspicuous (adj.)	Unit 8 Lesson A
cardiac (adj.)	Unit 4 Lesson A	controversy (n) (c)	Unit 9 Lesson B
cardiologist (n) (c)	Unit 4 Lesson A	construct (v) (T)	Unit 8 Lesson B
cardiology (n) (u)	Unit 4 Lesson A	construe (v) (T)	Unit 8 Lesson B
cardiovascular system	Unit 4 Lesson A	contact (n) (c) (v) (T)	Unit 6 Lesson A
centenary (n) (c)	Unit 1 Lesson B	contagious (adj.)	Unit 6 Lesson A
Centigrade (n) (c)	Unit 1 Lesson B	contemporary (adj.), (n)	Unit 3 Lesson A
centimetre (n) (c)	Unit 1 Lesson B	contortions (n) (plural)	Unit 8 Lesson B
centurion (n) (c)	Unit 1 Lesson B	contradict (v) (T)	Unit 5 Lesson A
century (n) (c)	Unit 1 Lesson B	contrast (n) (c) (V (T)	Unit 5 Lesson A
chlorine (n) (c)	Unit 7 Lesson A	contravene (v) (T)	Unit 5 Lesson A
chloroform (n) (u)	Unit 7 Lesson A	contretemps (n) (c)	Unit 5 Lesson A
chromium (n) (u)	Unit 7 Lesson A	contribute (v) (T)	Unit 9 Lesson B
chronic (adj.)	Unit 3 Lesson A	controversy (n) (c)	Unit 5 Lesson A
chronological (adj.)	Unit 3 Lesson A	curvilinear (adj.)	Unit 2 Lesson A

cyan (adj.)	Unit 7 Lesson A
cyanide (n) (u)	Unit 7 Lesson A
cyclical (adj.)	Unit 7 Lesson B
cyclone (n) (c)	Unit 7 Lesson B

D

decade (n) (c)	Unit 1 Lesson A
December (n) (u)	Unit 1 Lesson A
decibel (n) (c)	Unit 1 Lesson A
deciduous (adj.)	Unit 9 Lesson A
decimate (v) (T)	Unit 1 Lesson A
deduce (v) (T)	Unit 9 Lesson B
deodorant (n) (u)	Unit 6 Lesson A
deflect (v) (T)	Unit 2 Lesson A
deform (v) (T)	Unit 8 Lesson A
delineate (v) (T)	Unit 2 Lesson A
denigrate (v) (T)	Unit 7 Lesson A
dentures (n) (plural)	Unit 4 Lesson A
dermatologist (n) (c)	Unit 4 Lesson A
dermatitis (n) (u)	Unit 4 Lesson A
destruction (n) (u)	Unit 8 Lesson B
desultory (adj.)	Unit 9 Lesson B
detract (v) (T)	Unit 8 Lesson B
diagonal (adj.), (n) (c)	Unit 2 Lesson A
discoloured (adj.)	Unit 7 Lesson A
dismiss (v) (T)	Unit 8 Lesson B
dispassionate (adj.)	Unit 8 Lesson A
distort (v) (T)	Unit 8 Lesson B
distract (v) (T)	Unit 8 Lesson A
dynamic (adj.)	Unit 10 Lesson A
dynamo (n) (c)	Unit 10 Lesson A
dysentery (n) (u)	Unit 5 Lesson B
dysfunctional (adj.)	Unit 5 Lesson B
dyslexia (n) (c)	Unit 5 Lesson B
dyspepsia (n) (u)	Unit 5 Lesson B
dystopia (n) (c)	Unit 5 Lesson B

E

ego (n) (c)	Unit 6 Lesson B
egotistical (adj.)	Unit 6 Lesson B
ego trip (n) (c)	Unit 6 Lesson B
egocentric (adj.)	Unit 6 Lesson B
eject (v) (T)	Unit 9 Lesson B
elevate (v) (T)	Unit 9 Lesson A
emigrate (v) (T)	Unit 8 Lesson A
émigré (n) (c)	Unit 8 Lesson A
empathy (n) (u)	Unit 6 Lesson B
enamour (v) (T)	Unit 6 Lesson B
encircle (v) (T)	Unit 2 Lesson A
equality (n) (u)	Unit 10 Lesson B
equator (n) (u)	Unit 10 Lesson B
equidistant (adj.)	Unit 10 Lesson B
equilibrium (n) (u)	Unit 10 Lesson B
equivalent (adj.) (n) (c)	Unit 10 Lesson B
equivocal (adj.)	Unit 10 Lesson B
erect (v) (T)	Unit 2 Lesson A
evacuate (v) (T)	Unit 10 Lesson A
exacerbate (v) (T)	Unit 10 Lesson A
exalt (v) (T)	Unit 9 Lesson B
exhibit (v) (T)	Unit 9 Lesson A
exhume (v) (T)	Unit 19 Lesson B
export (v) (T)	Unit 7 Lesson B
extort (v) (T)	Unit 8 Lesson B

F

flexible (adj.)	Unit 2 Lesson A
formula (n) (c)	Unit 8 Lesson A
formulate (v) (T)	Unit 8 Lesson A
forte (n) (u)	Unit 10 Lesson A
fortify (v) (I)	Unit 10 Lesson A
fortitude (n) (u)	Unit 10 Lesson A
fraternal (adj.)	Unit 4 Lesson B
fraternity (n) (c)	Unit 4 Lesson B
geriatric (adj.)	Unit 4 Lesson B
grave (n) (c) (adj.)	Unit 10 Lesson A
gravitate (v) (T)	Unit 10 Lesson A
grief (n) (u)	Unit 10 Lesson A

grievance (n) (c)	Unit 10 Lesson A

H

habitat (n) (c)	Unit 9 Lesson A
hedonism (n) (u)	Unit 10 Lesson A
helicopter (n) (c)	Unit 7 Lesson B
helix (n) (c)	Unit 7 Lesson B
hesitate (v) (I)	Unit 9 Lesson B
heterodox (adj.)	Unit 4 Lesson B
heterogeneous (adj.)	Unit 4 Lesson B
hexagonal (adj.)	Unit 1 Lesson B
homeopathy (n) (u)	Unit 6 Lesson B
homogeneous (adj.)	Unit 4 Lesson B
homogenous (adj.)	Unit 4 Lesson B
homonym (n) (c)	Unit 4 Lesson B
hostile (adj.)	Unit 6 Lesson B
hostilities (n) (plural)	Unit 6 Lesson B
hype (n) (u)	Unit 2 Lesson B
hyperactive (adj.)	Unit 2 Lesson B
hypermarket (n) (c)	Unit 2 Lesson B
hypertension (n) (u)	Unit 2 Lesson B
hyperventilate (n) (m)	Unit 2 Lesson B

I

identical (adj.)	Unit 10 Lesson B
identify (v) (T)	Unit 10 Lesson B
idiomatic (adj.)	Unit 10 Lesson B
idiosyncrasy (n) (c)	Unit 10 Lesson B
idiot (n) (c)	Unit 10 Lesson B
illegible (adj.)	Unit 5 Lesson B
illicit (adj.)	Unit 5 Lesson B
immigration (n) (u)	Unit 8 Lesson A
immobile (adj.)	Unit 5 Lesson B
immobilize (v) (T)	Unit 7 Lesson B
immortal (adj.)	Unit 4 Lesson B
immutable (adj.)	Unit 7 Lesson B
impair (v) (T)	Unit 5 Lesson B
impassioned (adj.)	Unit 8 Lesson A
imports (n) (plural)	Unit 7 Lesson B
impugn (v) (T)	Unit 10 Lesson A
incident (n) (c)	Unit 9 Lesson A
incisive (adj.)	Unit 9 Lesson B
indoctrinate (v) (T)	Unit 11 Lesson A
inept (adj.)	Unit 5 Lesson B
infanticide (n) (u)	Unit 5 Lesson A
inherent (adj.)	Unit 9 Lesson B
inject (v) (T)	Unit 9 Lesson B
induce (v) (T)	Unit 9 Lesson A
infrastructure (n) (c)	Unit 8 Lesson B
inhabit (v) (T)	Unit 9 Lesson A
inquiry (n) (c)	Unit 8 Lesson B
intercept (v) (T)	Unit 8 Lesson B
intermix (v) (I)	Unit 9 Lesson A
involuntary (adj.)	Unit 8 Lesson A
implausible (adj.)	Unit 5 Lesson B
inadmissible (adj.)	Unit 5 Lesson B
inflection (n) (c)	Unit 2 Lesson A
inflexible (adj.)	Unit 2 Lesson A
intact (adj.)	Unit 6 Lesson A
intermediate (adj.)	Unit 2 Lesson B
intermission (n) (c)	Unit 3 Lesson B
international (adj.)	Unit 3 Lesson B
interpersonal (adj.)	Unit 3 Lesson B
intersection (n) (c)	Unit 3 Lesson B
interval (n) (c)	Unit 3 Lesson B
intranet (n) (c)	Unit 3 Lesson B
intransitive (adj.)	Unit 3 Lesson B
intrapersonal (adj.)	Unit 3 Lesson B
intravenous (adj.)	Unit 3 Lesson B
introspective (adj.)	Unit 8 Lesson A
introvert (n) (c)	Unit 3 Lesson B
invariably (adv.)	Unit 10 Lesson B
irrational (adj.)	Unit 5 Lesson B
irresistible (adj.)	Unit 5 Lesson B
irresponsible (adj.)	Unit 5 Lesson B
isolated (adj.)	Unit 10 Lesson B
isosceles (adj.)	Unit 10 Lesson B
isometric (adj.)	Unit 10 Lesson B

isotonic (adj.)	Unit 10 Lesson B	megabyte (n) (c)	Unit 2 Lesson B
isotope (n) (c)	Unit 10 Lesson B	megalomania (n) (u)	Unit 2 Lesson B
		melancholy (n) (c) (adj.)	Unit 7 Lesson A
J		melanin (n) (u)	Unit 7 Lesson A
juvenile (adj.) (n) (c)	Unit 4 Lesson B	melanoma (n) (c)	Unit 7 Lesson A
		melodrama (n) (c)	Unit 7 Lesson A
		microbe (n) (c)	Unit 2 Lesson B
K		microbiology (n) (u)	Unit 2 Lesson B
kilohertz (n) (c)	Unit 1 Lesson B	microchip (n) (c)	Unit 2 Lesson B
kilowatt (n) (c)	Unit 1 Lesson B	micrometre (n) (c)	Unit 2 Lesson A
L		microphone (n) (c)	Unit 6 Lesson B
leucine (n) (u)	Unit 7 Lesson A	microscopic (adj.)	Unit 2 Lesson B
leukaemia (n) (u)	Unit 7 Lesson A	middlebrow (adj.)	Unit 2 Lesson B
level-headed (adj.)	Unit 9 Lesson A	midway (adj.)	Unit 2 Lesson B
leverage (n) (u)	Unit 9 Lesson A	migrate (v) (T)	Unit 8 Lesson A
levitate (v) (T)	Unit 9 Lesson A	migratory (adj.)	Unit 8 Lesson A
lineage (n) (c)	Unit 2 Lesson A	millennium (n) (c)	Unit 1 Lesson B
locomotive (n) (c)	Unit 7 Lesson B	millibar (n) (c)	Unit 1 Lesson B
		millipede (n) (c)	Unit 1 Lesson B
		minimum (n) (u), (adj.)	Unit 2 Lesson B
M		miniskirt (n) (c)	Unit 2 Lesson B
macrocosm (n) (u)	Unit 2 Lesson B	miscegenation (n) (u)	Unit 9 Lesson A
macroeconomics (n) (u)	Unit 2 Lesson B	miniaturize (v) (T)	Unit 2 Lesson B
magnate (n) (c)	Unit 2 Lesson B	miscellaneous (adj.)	Unit 9 Lesson A
magnificent (adj.)	Unit 2 Lesson B	miscible (n) (u)	Unit 9 Lesson A
magnify (v) (T)	Unit 2 Lesson B	missile (n) (c)	Unit 8 Lesson B
malevolent (adj.)	Unit 8 Lesson A	missive (n) (c)	Unit 8 Lesson B
malodorous (adj.)	Unit 6 Lesson A	mission (n) (c)	Unit 8 Lesson B
manual (adj.) (n) (c)	Unit 4 Lesson A	mob (n) (c)	Unit 7 Lesson B
manufacture (v) (T)	Unit 4 Lesson A	mobile (adj.)	Unit 7 Lesson B
manuscript (n) (c)	Unit 4 Lesson A	mobility (n) (u)	Unit 7 Lesson B
maternal (adj.)	Unit 4 Lesson B	monarch (n) (c)	Unit 1 Lesson A
matriarchal (adj.)	Unit 4 Lesson B	monocycle (n) (c)	Unit 1 Lesson A
matrimony (n) (u)	Unit 4 Lesson B	monochrome (adj.)	Unit 7 Lesson A
matrix (n) (c)	Unit 4 Lesson B	monogamy (n) (u)	Unit 1 lesson A
matron (n) (c)	Unit 4 Lesson B	monoplane (n) (c)	Unit 1 Lesson A
mediate (v) (I)	Unit 2 Lesson B	monotheist (adj.)	Unit 1 Lesson A
mediocre (adj.)	Unit 2 Lesson B	morbid (adj.)	Unit 4 Lesson B
		mortality (n) (u)	Unit 4 Lesson B

motion (n) (c) (v) (T)	Unit 7 Lesson B	optician (n) (c)	Unit 4 Lesson A
motorize (v) (T)	Unit 7 Lesson B	oral (adj.)	Unit 4 Lesson A
multicoloured (adj.)	Unit 7 Lesson A	orifice (n) (c)	Unit 4 Lesson A
multicultural (adj.)	Unit 1 Lesson B	orthopaedic (adj.)	Unit 4 Lesson A
multifaceted (adj.)	Unit 1 Lesson B	orthodontics (n) (u)	Unit 4 Lesson A
multilateral (adj.)	Unit 1 Lesson B	osteopath (n) (c)	Unit 4 Lesson A
multi-storey (adj.)	Unit 1 Lesson B	osteoporosis (n) (u)	Unit 4 Lesson A
multitude (n) (c)	Unit 1 Lesson B	oval (n) (c), (adj.)	Unit 2 Lesson A
myocardium (n) (u)	Unit 4 Lesson A	ovulate (v) (I)	Unit 2 Lesson A

N

P

nascent (adj.)	Unit 4 Lesson B	pachyderm (n) (c)	Unit 4 Lesson A
nativity (n) (c) (adj.)	Unit 4 Lesson B	paediatric (adj.)	Unit 4 Lesson B
nausea (n) (u)	Unit 7 Lesson B	paediatrician (n) (c)	Unit 4 Lesson B
nautical (adj.)	Unit 7 Lesson B	passion (n) (c)	Unit 8 Lesson A
naval (adj.)	Unit 7 Lesson B	paternal (adj.)	Unit 4 Lesson B
navigate (v) (T)	Unit 7 Lesson B	paternity (n) (u)	Unit 4 Lesson B
negate (v) (T)	Unit 5 Lesson B	pathetic (adj.)	Unit 6 Lesson B
negativity (n) (u)	Unit 5 Lesson B	patient (adj.)	Unit 8 Lesson A
neurotic (adj.)	Unit 4 Lesson A	patriarchal (adj.)	Unit 4 Lesson B
neuralgia (n) (u)	Unit 4 Lesson A	patronage (n) (u)	Unit 4 Lesson B
neurosurgeon (n) (c)	Unit 4 Lesson A	patronising (adj.)	Unit 4 Lesson B
numerate (adj.)	Unit 1 Lesson B	pedestrian (n) (c)	Unit 4 Lesson A
		pedicure (n) (u)	Unit 4 Lesson A

O

		pentagon (n) (c)	Unit 2 Lesson A
		pentathlon (n) (c)	Unit 1 Lesson B
obdurate (adj.)	Unit 5 Lesson A	perceive (v) (T)	Unit 8 Lesson B
object (v) (T)	Unit 5 Lesson A	perennial (adj.)	Unit 3 Lesson A
obstruct (v) (T)	Unit 5 Lesson A	permanent (adj.)	Unit 3 Lesson A
octagonal (adj.)	Unit 2 Lesson A	pesticide (n) (c)	Unit 9 Lesson B
odour (n) (c)	Unit 6 Lesson A	pervade (v) (T)	Unit 13 Lesson A
odourless (adj.)	Unit 6 Lesson A	philanthropist (n) (c)	Unit 6 Lesson B
odoriferous (adj.)	Unit 6 Lesson A	philistine (n) (c)	Unit 6 Lesson B
omnibus (n) (c)	Unit 1 Lesson B	philharmonic (adj.)	Unit 6 Lesson B
omnipresent (adj.)	Unit 1 Lesson B	philosopher (n) (c)	Unit 10 Lesson A
omniscient (adj.)	Unit 1 Lesson B	philosophy (n) (u)	Unit 6 Lesson B
oppose (v) (T)	Unit 5 Lesson A	phonics (n) (u)	Unit 6 Lesson A
opposition (n) (u)	Unit 5 Lesson A	phonology (n) (u)	Unit 6 Lesson A

physics (n) (u)	Unit 4 Lesson A
physician (n) (c)	Unit 4 Lesson A
physique (n) (c)	Unit 4 Lesson A
polygon (n) (c)	Unit 2 Lesson A
port (n) (c)	Unit 7 Lesson B
portable (adj.)	Unit 7 Lesson B
postgraduate (n) (c)	Unit 3 Lesson A
postpone (v) (T)	Unit 3 Lesson A
posthumous (adj.)	Unit 3 Lesson A
postscript (n) (c)	Unit 3 Lesson A
post-war (adj.)	Unit 3 Lesson A
precedent (n) (c)	Unit 3 Lesson A
precise (adj.)	Unit 9 Lesson B
predict (v) (T)	Unit 3 Lesson A
preface (n) (c)	Unit 3 Lesson A
prerequisite (n) (c)	Unit 8 Lesson B
preserve (v) (T)	Unit 8 Lesson B
previous (adj.)	Unit 3 Lesson A
pre-war (adj.)	Unit 3 Lesson A
probability (n) (u)	Unit 5 Lesson B
probate (n) (c)	Unit 5 Lesson B
probation (n) (u)	Unit 5 Lesson B
probe (v) (T)	Unit 5 Lesson A
prohibit (v) (T)	Unit 9 Lesson A
projectile (n) (c)	Unit 9 Lesson B
proponent (n) (c)	Unit 5 Lesson A
propose (v) (T)	Unit 5 Lesson A
proposition (n) (c)	Unit 5 Lesson A
prospective (adj.)	Unit 8 Lesson A
psychologist (n) (c)	Unit 4 Lesson A
psychometric (adj.)	Unit 4 Lesson A
psychotherapy (n) (u)	Unit 15 Lesson B
pugilism (n) (u)	Unit 10 Lesson A
pungent (adj.)	Unit 10 Lesson A
pugnacious (adj.)	Unit 10 Lesson A
pyrrhic (adj.)	Unit 7 Lesson A

Q

quadrangle (n) (c)	Unit 1 Lesson A
quadrilateral (n) (c)	Unit 1 Lesson A
quadruped (n) (c)	Unit 1 Lesson A
quadruple (v) (T), (adj.)	Unit 1 Lesson A
quartet (n) (c)	Unit 1 Lesson A
quintessence (n) (u)	Unit 1 Lesson B
quintile (adj.)	Unit 1 Lesson B

R

realign (v) (T)	Unit 2 Lesson A
recipient (n) (c)	Unit 8 Lesson B
rectangular (adj.)	Unit 2 Lesson A
reflect (v) (T)	Unit 2 Lesson A
reform (v) (T)	Unit 8 Lesson A
regiment (n) (c), (v) (T)	Unit 2 Lesson A
rehabilitate (v) (T)	Unit 9 Lesson A
reign (v) (T) (n) (c)	Unit 12 Lesson A
rejuvenate (adj.)	Unit 4 Lesson B
remix (v) (T)	Unit 9 Lesson A
renegade (n) (c)	Unit 5 Lesson B
renege (v) (T)	Unit 5 Lesson B
reporter (n) (c)	Unit 7 Lesson B
reprove (v) (T)	Unit 5 Lesson B
repugnant (adj.)	Unit 10 Lesson A
requisition (n) (c) (v) (T)	Unit 8 Lesson B
reservation (n) (c)	Unit 8 Lesson B
resent (v) (T)	Unit 6 Lesson B
resilience (n) (u)	Unit 9 Lesson B
retort (v) (T)	Unit 8 Lesson B
retrofit (v) (T)	Unit 3 Lesson A
retrograde (adj.)	Unit 3 Lesson A
retrospectively (adv.)	Unit 3 Lesson A
retro style (adj.)	Unit 3 Lesson A
rhododendron (n) (c)	Unit 7 Lesson A
rubella (n) (c)	Unit 7 Lesson A
ruby (n) (c) (adj.)	Unit 7 Lesson A

S

sapphire (n) (c) (adj.)	Unit 7 Lesson A
scissors (n) (plural)	Unit 9 Lesson B
seduce (v) (T)	Unit 9 Lesson A
sensitive (adj.)	Unit 6 Lesson B
sentimentally (adv.)	Unit 6 Lesson B
servile (adj.)	Unit 8 Lesson B
sexagenarian (n) (c)	Unit 1 Lesson B
somersault (n) (c)	Unit 9 Lesson B
sophisticated (adj.)	Unit 10 Lesson A
sophistry (n) (u)	Unit 10 Lesson A
Sophists (n) (plural)	Unit 10 Lesson A
sophomore (n) (c)	Unit 10 Lesson A
sorority (n) (c)	Unit 4 Lesson B
spectator (n) (c) (adj.)	Unit 8 Lesson A
structure (n) (c) (v) (T)	Unit 8 Lesson B
subconscious (adj.)	Unit 3 Lesson B
subjunctive (n) (u)	Unit 3 Lesson B
submerge (v) (T)	Unit 3 Lesson B
subordinate (n) (c)(adj.)	Unit 3 Lesson B
subservient (adj.)	Unit 8 Lesson B
substandard (adj.)	Unit 3 Lesson B
superior (adj.) (n) (c)	Unit 3 Lesson B
superb (adj.)	Unit 3 Lesson B
superfluous (adj.)	Unit 3 Lesson B
supervise (v) (T)	Unit 3 Lesson B
supersonic (adj.)	Unit 3 Lesson B
syllogism (n) (c)	Unit 10 Lesson B
symmetrical (adj.)	Unit 10 Lesson B
sympathetically (adv.)	Unit 6 Lesson B
symphony (n) (c)	Unit 6 Lesson A
synchronize (v) (T)	Unit 3 Lesson A
synchronous (adj.)	Unit 10 Lesson B
synergy (n) (c)	Unit 10 Lesson B
synonym (n) (c)	Unit 10 Lesson B

T

tactile (adj.)	Unit 6 Lesson A
tangible (adj.)	Unit 6 Lesson A
telecommunications (n)	Unit 3 Lesson B
telecommuting (n) (c)	Unit 3 Lesson B
telemetry (n) (u)	Unit 3 Lesson B
telepathy (n) (u)	Unit 3 Lesson B
telescope (n) (c)	Unit 3 Lesson B
temporal (adj.)	Unit 3 Lesson A
temporary (adj.)	Unit 3 Lesson A
torsion (n) (u)	Unit 8 Lesson B
tricycle (n) (c)	Unit 7 Lesson B
tract (n) (c)	Unit 8 Lesson A
traction (n) (u)	Unit 8 Lesson A
tractor (n) (c)	Unit 8 Lesson A
trajectory (n) (c)	Unit 9 Lesson B
transnational (adj.)	Unit 3 Lesson B
transcript (n) (c)	Unit 3 Lesson B
transport (n) (u), (v) (T)	Unit 3 Lesson B
transparent (adj.)	Unit 3 Lesson B
transpose (v) (T)	Unit 3 Lesson B
transverse (adj.)	Unit 9 Lesson B
triangle (n) (c)	Unit 1 Lesson A
tribulation (n) (c)	Unit 9 Lesson B
tributary (n) (c)	Unit 9 Lesson B
tribute (n) (c)	Unit 9 Lesson B
trigonometry (n) (u)	Unit 2 Lesson A
triplicate (n) (c), (v) (T)	Unit 1 Lesson A
tripod (n) (c)	Unit 1 Lesson A
Trinity (n) (u)	Unit 1 Lesson A
triumvirate (n) (c)	Unit 1 Lesson A

U

ultimate (adj.)	Unit 2 Lesson B
ultimatum (n) (c)	Unit 2 Lesson B
ultramodern (adj.)	Unit 2 Lesson B
ultrasound scan (n) (c)	Unit 2 Lesson B
ultraviolet (adj.)	Unit 2 Lesson B
uniform (n) (c)	Unit 1 Lesson A
unify (v) (T)	Unit 1 Lesson A
unilateral (adj.)	Unit 1 Lesson A

unique (adj.)	Unit 1 Lesson A
university (n) (c)	Unit 1 Lesson A

V

vacant (adj.)	Unit 10 Lesson A
vacation (n) (c)	Unit 10 Lesson A
vacuous (adj.)	Unit 10 Lesson A
vacuum (n) (c)	Unit 10 Lesson A
variance (n) (c)	Unit 10 Lesson B
variegate (v) (T)	Unit 10 Lesson B
variety (n) (c)	Unit 10 Lesson B
various (adj.)	Unit 10 Lesson B
versatile (adj.)	Unit 9 Lesson B
video (n) (c)	Unit 6 Lesson A
visage (n) (c)	Unit 6 Lesson A
visibility (n) (u)	Unit 6 Lesson A
vista (n) (c)	Unit 6 Lesson A
visual (adj.)	Unit 6 Lesson A
vocal (adj.)	Unit 6 Lesson A
vocabulary (n) (u)	Unit 6 Lesson A
vociferous (adj.)	Unit 6 Lesson A
vocalize (v) (T)	Unit 6 Lesson A
voluntary (adj.)	Unit 8 Lesson A
volunteer (n) (c)	Unit 8 Lesson A
volition (n) (u)	Unit 8 Lesson A

Printed in Great Britain
by Amazon